VIVIAN HØXBRO'S
KNITTING HANDBOOK

VIVIAN HØXBRO'S

KNITTING HANDBOOK

8 SCHOOLS OF MODULAR KNITTING

Trafalgar Square
North Pomfret, Vermont

Vivian Høxbro

Vivian Høxbro has worked as a knitting designer for over 35 years, both for yarn companies and freelance. She has written 12 knitting books, some of which were published in Norway, Japan, and the United States. In 2000, she presented her own kit collection. Since then, she has taught and given lectures in Scandinavia as well as in the U. S. and Japan. She is now working to make Denmark's first knitting museum in Stubbekøbing a reality.

www.viv.dk

She is also the author of *Traditional Danish Sweaters*, available from Trafalgar Square Books.

First published in the United States of America
in 2022 by
Trafalgar Square Books
North Pomfret, Vermont 05053

Originally published in Danish as *Finurlig strik*.

The instructions and material lists in this book were carefully reviewed by the author and editor; however, accuracy cannot be guaranteed. The author and publisher cannot be held liable for errors.

ISBN: 978-1-64601-135-3
Library of Congress Control Number: 2022930196

Text and Pattern Design: Vivian Høxbro (www.viv.dk)
Charts: Design Partner (www.design-partner.dk)
Photos: Ingrid Riis (www.ingridriisfotografi.dk)
Step-by-Step Photos: Vivian Høxbro
Stylist and Color Consultant: Sophia Høxbro
Danish Editor: Merete Kjær Petersen
Interior Graphic Design: Karin Hold
Cover Design: RM Didier
Translation into English: Carol Huebscher Rhoades

Printed in China
10 9 8 7 6 5 4 3 2 1

TABLE OF CONTENTS

PREFACE

Knitting strips, squares, and other shapes that are joined as you work or crocheted together afterwards is enjoyable and motivating. All the while, you'll be well-entertained, which is exactly what knitting means to me.

When I was a child (right after WWII), people would unravel old sweaters and knit new ones from the salvaged yarn. Of course, back then, everyone needed warm clothes and they could be hard to come by. I remember one sweater with Norwegian patterning in blue and yellow—I hated it! It isn't the same these days, when most people have so many clothes that they could fill a whole separate room with them.

KNITTING AND PLEASURE

Let's be realistic: The vast majority of us no longer knit out of necessity but for enjoyment. That doesn't mean that we can't refine our skills and enjoy learning! The more you know, the better the results, and the happier you will be about the work.

I have never been a fan of "cast on 385 stitches and knit around to the underarms," etc. Knitting something for yourself that could just as easily be bought, and probably more cheaply than your yarn, isn't my idea of a good time. I'd rather be entertained and challenged, and create something you could never find in a store. I like the knitting process.

If you also feel that way, or you'd like a change of pace from your usual patterns, then this book is for you.

LEARN NEW TECHNIQUES—8 "SCHOOLS"

You are undoubtedly familiar with some of the techniques in this book because they build on domino knitting. You can learn the techniques you don't already know if you follow the book's 8 "schools," which is to say the 8 categories, organized by shape, that I've divided these pattern techniques into. Spend a few evenings studying each school, preferably with your knitting friends. It's always great to work together so you can help each other.

If you like to teach, you'll also find teaching materials here, ready to use. I would, of course, be happy if you encouraged your students to buy the book.

I would like to recommend that you save the "Staircase" school for last. It isn't especially difficult, but it uses some of the techniques presented in the other schools, so studying the rest first will make the instructions easier to follow. The Staircase technique is simpler than it looks, and once you've gone through the other schools, it will be like a game—entertaining and motivating. I'm wild about it, as you'll see from the patterns that make use of it.

PATTERNS—16 DESIGNS

Each of the 8 "schools" includes two designs, which expand on the fundamental knitting technique presented in each respective school. Once you've learned each technique, you can follow the patterns and even design your own, combining or rearranging the building blocks from each school.

COLORS

If you've encountered any of my designs before, you know that I go all out on the color palette. This time, I listened to my creative granddaughter, Sophia. She has been my consultant, and she inspired me to refresh my style and step into a new color world. It is also Sophia who was the book's stylist, and her school friends joined in as the book's models! Thank you, Sophia!

PICTURES AND TEXT

"My" photographer, Ingrid Riis, and Sophia and I totally agreed that we wanted to show how beautiful it is on Østfalster at the Corselitze estate's forest and accompanying lake, which spills out into the Øster Sea. We photographed on the warmest day of summer, so everything looked its most beautiful. Thank you, Corselitze.

I would also like to thank my Danish publisher, Turbine. This is the third book we've published together. I'm very thankful for the publisher's openness and accommodation, which allowed me to work on exactly the books I wanted to publish. And thank you to Trafalgar Square Books for taking on the task of publishing this book in English!

In addition, I want to thank my Danish editor, Merete Kjær Petersen. If you have had Merete as your editor, you know how much work and enthusiasm she puts into her editing and the close collaboration we had during the editing process. It is her participation that gave my book precisely the degree of quality I wished for. Many, many thanks, Merete!

KNITTING HANDBOOK

With this book, I am sharing my methods of knitting with you. My dream is that you will play and experiment further, as you may already have played with regular domino knitting. Above all, I want to spread happiness and excitement about knitting, with the many possibilities there are to enjoy working with yarn and needles.

Knitting Greetings from
Vivian Høxbro
www.viv.dk

MATERIALS

YARN

Some of the patterns and all of the swatches in this book were knitted with Pernilla from Filcolana, a wool yarn that knits up evenly and beautifully. This "mélange" yarn shifts to heather shades, usually with a bit of white.

When I wanted a particularly delicate, thin yarn in soft colors, I chose Isager yarns. In addition, I enjoyed working with Hedgehog Kidsilk Lace—the finest hand-dyed silk mohair from Ireland.

NEEDLES

For the knitting in this book, I used double-pointed needles, hybrid jumper needles, and circular needles. I changed from double points to a circular as I worked, whenever it was practical and comfortable.

My needles of choice are Ferrari ChiaoGoo circulars with points made with surgical steel. However, everyone has their own favorites, of course. It's easiest to knit slick yarns— such as Tilia from Filcolana, Isager Silk Mohair, and Hedgehog's Kidsilk Lace, for example—with wooden needles, so the stitches won't slide off the needles.

For certain finishing jobs, it's a good idea to have a good crochet hook on hand.

Small, soft ring markers

Locking ring stitch markers

Stitch stoppers

Small elastic cords

TOOLS

It's important to have your tools organized. Besides knitting needles and crochet hooks, you should also have a good pair of scissors and a blunt tapestry needle for joining.

Personally, I can't live without locking ring stitch markers. My knitting life certainly became easier when I found these small ring markers from the Japanese company Clover. They're similar to safety pins, and can be used to mark increases and decreases as you work. Other markers that should be in your notions bag include small soft rings (mine are also from Clover).

Other useful tools include various lengths of yarn, mostly 6-8 in / 15-20 cm long, stitch stoppers (also see page 185) as well as small rubber bands (mine are from Panduro Hobby) for marking increases and decreases and to place on needle tips—I use these when taking a knitting project out into the world.

BEFORE YOU KNIT
Explanations at the back of this book:
Techniques and abbreviations used in the book are explained under Basic Techniques, Knitting Help (alphabetized list), or in Abbreviations. **Read through these sections carefully before you begin knitting!**

Text in Italics
In Schools 2, 4, 5, and 6, and in the accompanying patterns, some motifs are worked alternately in knits and purls. To make it easier to navigate the pattern, the instructional text is in regular and italic print respectively—for example:
Motifs to be **knitted** are in regular text.
*Motifs to be **purled** are in italics.*

SCHOOLS
AND
DESIGNS

1
STRIPES

STRIPES

Stripes can be knitted either vertically or horizontally with an easy technique that is endlessly variable. Begin with a strip of 8 stitches and 50 garter ridges. On the right side of the strip, work an intermediate middle stripe with 50 stitches and 12 rows (= 6 garter ridges) and then work 1 strip parallel to the first one and along the stitches of the intermediate stripe.

FINISHED MEASUREMENTS

Width: 7½ in / 19 cm
Length: 8 in / 20 cm
Each Strip: approx. 1¼ x 8 in / 3 x 20 cm

MATERIALS

Yarn: CYCA #3 (DK, light worsted)
Filcolana Pernilla (100% pure new wool, 191 yd/175 m / 50 g)
Colors:
Isabella Heather 820 (pink)
Acacia Heather 825 (curry)
Charcoal Heather 956 (charcoal)
Marzipan Heather 977 (natural white)

Needles: U. S. size 2.5 / 3 mm: 2 dpn

SWATCH

Stitch Count

In principle, the strips can have any number of stitches and rows, but the final number of garter ridges and intermediate stripes should always be the same. Each strip here has 8 sts and 50 garter ridges (= 100 knit rows). The intermediate stripes have 50 sts.

1ST STRIP

Worked **horizontally** with pink.

K-CO 8 sts (with 2 beg sts) on a dpn.
Row 1 (RS): Knit across.
Row 2 (WS): Sl 1 pwise, knit to end of row.
Row 3 (RS): Sl 1 pwise, knit to end of row.
Rep Rows 2-3 until there are

49 ridges on RS and you've just completed a RS row. The yarn hangs on left side.
BO on WS; cut yarn, elongate the 8th st and draw yarn end through it (end st), but do not tighten st. There are now 50 ridges on RS and WS. The yarn end from the cast-on hangs at left side and the yarn from the bind-off is on the right side (see photo A).

1ST INTERMEDIATE STRIPE

Work vertically, alternating 2 rows charcoal and 2 rows natural white.
Work all color changes on RS rows; the last row is on WS.

Row 1 (RS), pick up and knit:
With charcoal, pick up and knit 1 st in loop of 1st strip's lower right corner, and then pick up and knit

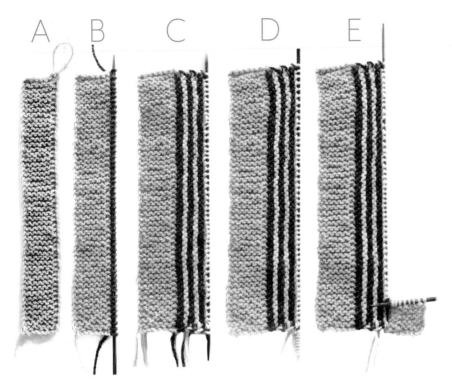

A   B   C   D   E

A Narrow or Nonexistent Intermediate Stripe

You can settle for just one vertical row as a vertical intermediate stripe—it will look like lovely stitching. Be aware, though, that in order to avoid a notch on the piece's edge, you must pick up and knit 2 more stitches than needed. You can knit them together on the next row. See Spiral Top on page 25.

sts along the right side (1 st in each ridge). End with k1 in end st (= 52) sts. These horizontal sts are the intermediate stripe sts (ISS).

There are now 2 sts more than ridges or edge sts. These sts prevent a "notch" at bottom and top, and will be decreased on Row 2.
Row 2 (WS): Sl 1 pwise, k2tog, knit until 3 sts rem, k2tog, p1.
Now the extra sts have been removed (photo B). Change to natural white.
Row 3: Sl 1 kwise, knit to end of row.
Row 4: Sl 1 pwise, knit to last st, p1. Hold charcoal out under/in front of and over natural white (see Changing Colors with Stripes, page 174), slip first st kwise and then continue with charcoal. Do not tighten yarns when changing colors!
Row 5: Sl 1 kwise, knit to end of row.
Row 6: Sl 1 pwise, knit to last st, p1. Hold natural white out under/in front of and over charcoal, sl 1 kwise, and continue with natural white. Rep Rows 3-6 until there are 3 charcoal and 3 natural white ridges on RS (photo C). Weave in ends.

2ND STRIP

Worked **horizontally** with curry.

Use bottom st of intermediate stripe as beginning st and K-CO 8 sts as an extension of sts from intermediate stripe (photo D) = 50 + 8 sts on needle.
Row 1 (RS): K7, p2tog (= with 1 st from strip and 1 ISS); turn.
There are now 49 ISS + 8 curry sts.
Row 2 (WS): Sl 1 kwise, knit to end of row; turn.
Row 3: Sl 1 pwise, k6, p2tog; turn.
There are now 48 ISS + 8 curry sts.
Row 4: Sl 1 pwise, knit to end of row; turn.
Rep Rows 3-4 until 3 ISS rem after a WS row (photo E).
Next Row (RS): Sl 1 pwise, k6, p3tog; turn.
Next Row (WS): Sl 1 kwise, knit to end of row; turn
Next Row (RS): Sl 1 pwise, k6, p2tog; turn.
BO on WS, slipping 1st st pwise. Leave end st loose as on 1st strip. Cut yarn.
There are now 50 ridges on RS and WS.

2ND INTERMEDIATE STRIPE

Work as for 1st intermediate stripe.

3RD STRIP

Work as for 2nd strip, but with pink.

3RD INTERMEDIATE STRIPE

Work as for 1st intermediate stripe.

4TH STRIP

Work as for 2nd strip.

TRIANGULAR SHAWL

This distinctive shawl is an interplay of triangles and stripes. The shawl consists of 2 almost identical large triangles, knitted as extensions of each other.

FINISHED MEASUREMENTS
Width: wingspan, 74 in / 188 cm
Length: at center, 34¼ in / 87 cm

MATERIALS
Yarn: CYCA #0 (lace) Hedgehog Fibres Kidsilk Lace (70% kid mohair, 30% silk, 459 yd/420 m / 50 g)
Yarn Colors and Amounts:
Fool's Gold (yellow): 100 g
I purchased the Kidsilk Lace yarn for this shawl at www.tantegroencph.dk

Yarn: CYCA #0 (lace) Filcolana Tilia (70% superkid mohair, 30% mulberry silk, 230 yd/210 m / 25 g)
Yarn Colors and Amounts:
Purple 286 (gray-violet): 10 g
Peach Blossom 335 (salmon): 10 g

Needles: U. S. size 4 / 3.5 mm: 2 dpn and 24 in / 60 cm circular

Notions: locking ring stitch markers

GAUGE
20 sts and 44 rows/22 ridges with Kidsilk Lace = 4 x 4 in / 10 x 10 cm. Adjust needle size to obtain correct gauge if necessary.

INSTRUCTIONS

Technique
This pattern is based on School 1 (page 16) and the diagram on page 21. Learn the technique by knitting all of School 1 or only part of it.

Diagram
The diagram shows the 2 large triangles, each consisting of 4 figures. Turn the diagram as you work, so that the arrow in the figure you're working (which indicates knitting direction) points up.

Edge Stitches
All of the figures in this shawl have 2 edge stiches at the outer sides. Along the sides, where the figure is joined with the other sides, there is only 1 edge stitch.

1ST LARGE TRIANGLE
FIGURE 1
One triangle, which is straight up on the right side and has increases on the left side.

There should be 2 edge sts on each side.

With yellow and dpn, CO 2 sts.
Row 1 (RS): K2.
Row 2 (WS): Sl 1 pwise, increase 1 (see page 186), k1 (= 3 sts).
Row 3: Sl 1 pwise, k2.
Row 4: Sl 1 pwise, 1 inc, knit to end of row (= 4 sts).
Row 5: Sl 1 pwise, knit to end of row.
Row 6: Sl 2 pwise, 1 inc, k2 (= 5 sts).
Row 7: Sl 2 pwise, knit to end of row.
Row 8: Sl 2 pwise, 1 inc, knit to end of row (= 6 sts).
Rep Rows 7-8 with more and more sts. Change to U. S. 4 / 3.5 mm circular when comfortable and work back and forth.
End when there are 88 sts and after a WS row (= after a row with 1 increase). Do not cut yarn. The yarn hangs at the right side.

Eyelet Row
Change to gray-violet and work

2 more rows as before (= 89 sts).
Next Row (RS): Sl 2 pwise,
k2tog, yo; rep * to * until 3 sts
rem, k3.
Next Row (WS): Sl 2 pwise, 1
inc, knit to end of row (= 90 sts).
Cut yarn.

FIGURE 2

Begin with an edge strip, then a
rectangle, and finally a triangle.

NOTE: See Changing Color with
Stripes, page 174.

Edge Strip

Change back to yellow and, with
a dpn to help, knit in direction of
arrow over first 7 sts of Figure 1
(leave rem sts on circular).
Row 1 (RS): Sl 2 pwise, k5; turn.
Row 2 (WS): Sl 1 pwise, knit to
end of row; turn.
Rep Rows 1-2 until there are 29
ridges on RS.
Knit 1 row on RS. Do not cut yarn.

Rectangle
Row 1 (RS), pick up and knit:
Place bottom 6 sts of edge strip
on a holder for later. Knit the 7th
st and continue by picking up and
knitting 29 sts along edge strip,
move last st to left needle, p2tog
(= 30 sts); turn.
Row 2 (WS): Sl 1 kwise, knit to
last st, p1; turn.
Row 3 (RS): Sl 1 kwise,
k28, p2tog; turn.

Rep Rows 2-3 only once. Now rep
Rows 2-3 in stripes: alternate 4
rows with salmon and 4 rows with
yellow, until 1 st rem before eyelet
row. The last row is on RS and
ends with k2tog instead of p2tog
(= 30 sts rem).

Triangle

Continue in stripes. On the left
side (along diagonal), work
2 edge sts; inside edge sts,
decrease on RS.
Row 1 (WS): Sl 2 pwise, knit to
last st, p1.
Row 2 (RS): Sl 1 kwise, knit until
4 sts rem, k2tog, k2.
Rep Rows 1-2 until 4 sts rem after
a RS row.
Finish as:
Row 1 (WS): Sl 2 pwise, k1, p1.
Row 2 (RS): Sl 1 kwise, k2tog, k1.
Row 3: Sl 1 pwise, k2.
Row 4: Sl 1, k2 tog, psso.
Place last st on a locking ring
marker.
Cut yarn and weave in ends.

FIGURE 3

A triangle, beginning in
lower half of Figure 2.
Work 2 edge sts

on right side and 1 edge st on
left side.

Row 1 (RS), pick up and knit:

Move 6 held sts to circular and
knit them with yellow; continue
by picking up and knitting 54 sts
along right side of Figure 2
(= 60 sts).
Row 2 (WS): Sl 1 pwise, sl 1, k1,
psso, knit to end of row; turn.
Row 3 (RS): Sl 2 pwise, knit to
end of row; turn.
Rep Rows 2-3 until 4 sts rem after
a RS row.
Finish with:
Row 1 (WS): Sl 1
pwise, k2tog, k1; turn.
Row 2 (RS): Sl 1 pwise, k2
(= 3 sts); turn.
Do not cut yarn.

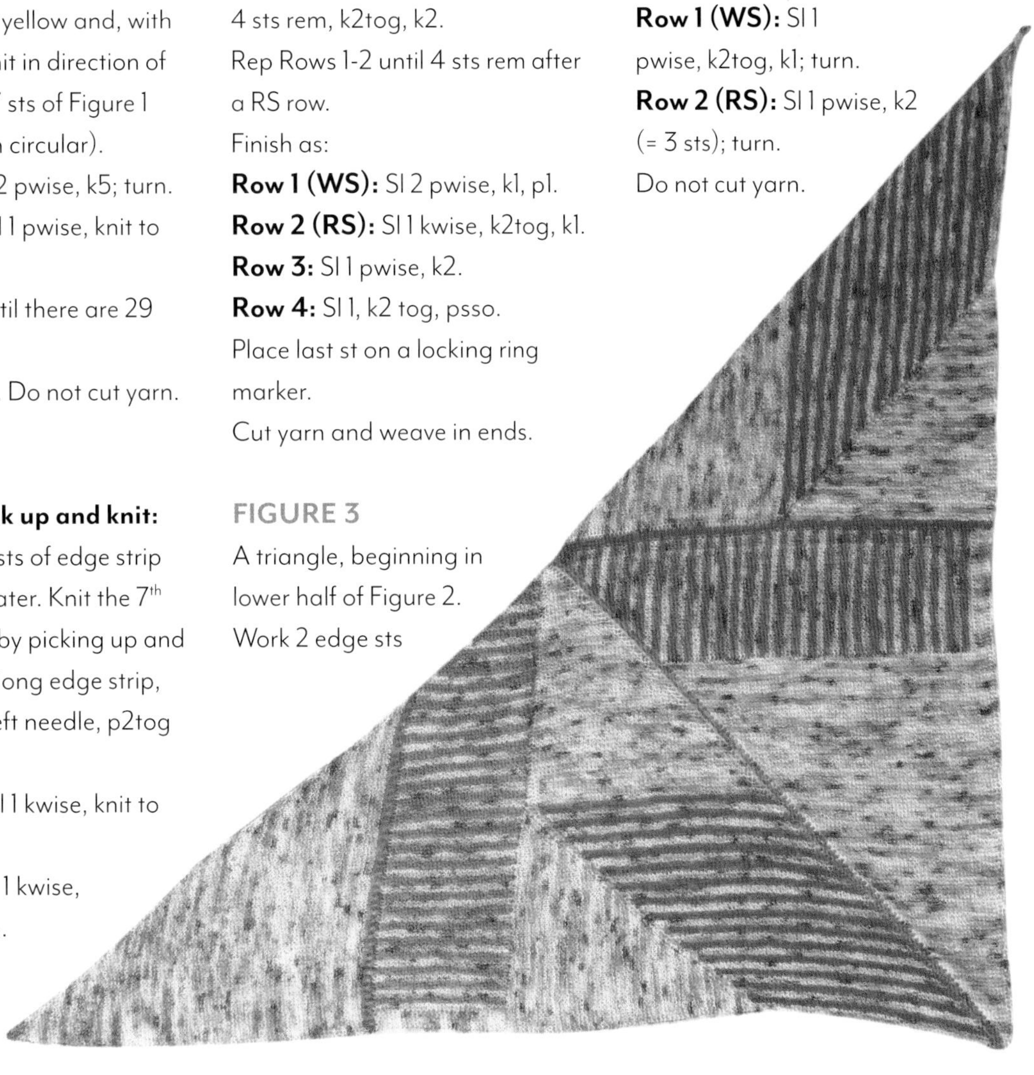

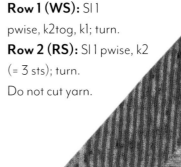

FIGURE 4

This figure is worked along Figures 2 and 3 in the direction indicated by the arrow. It begins with a single-color triangle along Figure 2 with increases on the left side and continues in stripes in a parallelogram on the diagonal along Figure 3. Work 1 edge stitch on both sides of the figure. The figure ends with an I-cord bind-off that looks like 2 edge stitches.

Triangle

Row 1 (RS), pick up and knit: Begin with the yarn from Figure 3. With circular, pick up and knit 60 sts along Figure 3 and 59 sts along Figure 2, and knit Figure 2's last st (on locking marker) (= 123 sts, including the 3 sts from Figure 3). The 120 sts will gradually be eliminated. Turn.

Row 2 (WS): K1 and k1tbl in same st (= 2 sts); turn.

Row 3: Sl 1 pwise, k1; turn.

Row 4: Sl 1 pwise, 1 inc, sl 1, k1, psso (= 3 sts); turn.

Row 5: Sl 1 pwise, k2; turn.

Row 6: Sl 1 pwise, 1 inc, k1, sl 1, k1, psso (= 4 sts); turn.

Row 7: Sl 1 pwise, knit to end of row; turn.

Row 8: Sl 1 pwise, 1 inc, k2, sl 1, k1, psso (= 5 sts); turn.

Row 9: Sl 1 pwise, knit to end of row; turn.

Row 10: Sl 1 pwise, 1 inc, k3, sl 1, k1, psso (= 6 sts); turn.

Rep Rows 9-10, with 1 more st on every WS row until there are 60 sts on the triangle after a WS row.

Parallelogram

Continue in stripes: alternate 4 rows with gray-violet and 4 rows with yellow, increasing and decreasing at the sides as follows:

Row 1 (RS): Sl 1 pwise, k2tog, knit to end of row; turn.

Row 2 (WS): Sl 1 pwise, 1 inc, k57, sl 1, k1, psso; turn.

Work all color changes before a RS row inside the work between Figures 3 and 4.

Rep Rows 1-2 until 60 sts rem from Figure 4 and 3 sts rem from Figure 3. The last row is on WS and ends when 5 sts rem, with sl 1, k1, psso, k3.

Now work edging:

I-cord bind-off:

Row 1 (RS): Sl 2 pwise, p2tog; turn.

Row 2 (WS): Sl 1 kwise, k2.

Rep Rows 1-2 until only 3 sts rem. Do not cut yarn.

EYELET ROW IN MIDDLE OF SHAWL

This eyelet row is indicated with a red line on the diagram. Change to salmon.

Row 1 (RS), pick up and knit: With circular, sl 2 pwise, k1, pick up and knit 117 sts along Figure 4 (= 120 sts).

Row 2 (WS): Sl 1 pwise, knit to end of row.

Row 3: Sl 2 pwise *k2tog, yo*; rep from * to * until 2 sts rem, k2.

Row 4: Sl 2 pwise, knit to end of row.

2ND LARGE TRIANGLE
FIGURE 5

Corresponds to Figure 1 but is knitted together with and as a continuation of the 1st large triangle.

With yellow, K-CO with 2 sts, where the eyelet row ended, and knit a triangle as follows:

Row 1 (RS): Sl 2 pwise; turn.

Row 2 (WS): K2.

Row 3: Sl 2 pwise, 1 inc; turn.

Row 4: Sl 1 pwise, knit to end of row.

Row 5: Sl 2 pwise, 1 inc, p2tog (= 4 sts); turn.

Row 6: Sl 1 kwise, knit to end of row.

Row 7: Sl 2 pwise, k2-in-1, p2tog (= 5 sts); turn.

Row 8: Sl 1 kwise, knit to end of row.

Row 9: Sl 2 pwise, k1, k2-in-1, p2tog (= 6 sts); turn.

Row 10 (WS): Sl 1 kwise, knit to end of row.

Row 11 (RS): Sl 2 pwise, k2, k2-in-1, p2tog (= 7 sts); turn.

Rep Row 10-11 until there are 90 sts; Figure 5 will have more and more sts. End with a WS row. Do not cut yarn. Omit eyelet row here.

FIGURE 6

There should now be 120 sts on the needle: 30 salmon and 90 yellow sts.

Work an edge strip as in Figure 2. Continue with a rectangle as for Figure 2 until 30 salmon sts and 1 yellow st rem. End last row on RS with p2tog.

Triangle

The triangle is shaped with decreases on the left side and 1 edge st on the right side as follows:

WS Rows: Sl 1 kwise, knit to last st, p1.

RS Rows: Sl 1 kwise, knit to last 3 sts of triangle k2tog, p2tog (work p2tog with 1 st of triangle and 1 st of eyelet row); turn.

When 3 sts on triangle and 3 sts on eyelet row rem, end as follows:

Row 1 (RS): Sl 1 kwise, k1, p3tog, p1.

Row 2 (WS): Sl 1 kwise, k2, p1.

Row 3: Sl 1 kwise, k3tog, pass slipped st over the 3 tog. Place last st on a locking marker. Cut yarn and weave in end.

Eyelet Row

Change to gray-violet.

Row 1 (RS), pick up and knit: With circular, pick up and knit 120 sts along right side of Figure 6, including 6 edge sts and 1 st held on marker.

Row 2 (WS): Sl 1 kwise, knit to end of row.

Row 3: Sl 2 pwise *k2tog, yo*; rep from * to * until 2 sts rem, k2.

Row 4: Sl 2 pwise, knit to end of row.

Cut yarn and weave in end.

FIGURE 7

Work as for Figure 3, but work Row 1 as follows: Sl 1 kwise, k59 (= 60 sts). Leave rem 60 sts on needle for Figure 8.

FIGURE 8

This figure corresponds to Figure 4 but is knitted with 2 edge sts on left side, where sts are not joined.

Triangle

Row 1 (RS), pick up and knit: With circular, begin with the 3 sts and yarn from Figure 7 and, with yellow, pick up and knit 60 sts along Figure 7 and 59 sts along Figure 6; knit last st of Figure 6 (held on marker) (= 123 sts). The 120 sts will gradually be eliminated. Turn.

Row 2 (WS): P1 and k1tbl in same st (= 2 sts); turn.

Row 3: Sl 1 pwise, k1; turn.

Row 4: Sl 1 pwise, 1 inc, sl 1, k1, psso (= 3 sts); turn.

Row 5: Sl 1 pwise, k2; turn.

Row 6: Sl 2 pwise, 1 inc, sl 1, k1, psso (= 4 sts); turn.

Row 7 (and all following RS rows): Sl 1 pwise, knit to end of row; turn.

Row 8: Sl 2 pwise, 1 inc, k1, sl 1, k1, psso (= 5 sts); turn.

Row 10: Sl 2 pwise, 1 inc 1, k2, sl 1, k1, psso (= 6 sts); turn.

Continue by increasing 1 st after the 2 edge sts (sl 2 pwise) on all WS rows and end with sl 1, k1,

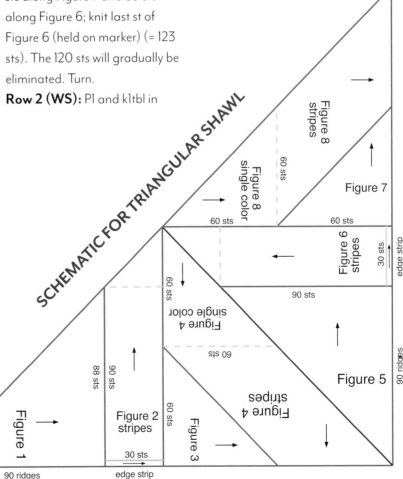

SCHEMATIC FOR TRIANGULAR SHAWL

Figure 1

Figure 2 stripes

Figure 3

Figure 4 stripes

Figure 4 single color

Figure 5

Figure 6 stripes

Figure 7

Figure 8 single color

Figure 8 stripes

90 ridges

edge strip

88 sts

90 sts

30 sts

60 sts

60 sts

60 sts

60 sts

30 sts

90 sts

60 sts

60 sts

90 sts

edge strip

90 ridges

psso until there are 60 sts after a WS row.

Parallelogram

Continue in stripes: alternate 4 rows with gray-violet and 4 rows with yellow, increasing and decreasing at the sides as follows:

Row 1 (RS): Sl 1 pwise, k2tog, knit to end of row; turn.

Row 2 (WS): Sl 2 pwise, 1 inc, k57, sl 1, k1, psso; turn.

Work all color changes inside the work between Figures 7 and 8.

Rep Rows 1-2 until 60 sts rem from Figure 8 and 3 sts rem from Figure 7 after a WS row. These 3 rem sts = RS row. Cut yarn and go to these sts.

I-cord bind-off:

Row 1 (WS): K3 from Figure 7.

Row 2 (RS): Sl 2 pwise, p2tog; turn.

Sl 1 kwise, k2.

Rep Rows 2-3 until 4 sts rem. Do not cut yarn.

Bind-Off

You could bind off with k2tog twice and then pass 1st st over 2nd. I decided to end with a little cord:

Row 1: K1, sl 1 pwise, k1, sl 1 pwise; turn.

Rep this row until cord is about 2 in / 5 cm long.

Finish as follows: K2tog, k2tog, pass 1st st over 2nd and draw yarn end though st. Cut yarn and weave in ends; tie knot.

SPIRAL TOP

This top is asymmetrical and unusual, but it's not difficult to knit. It begins with a very long strip of wide and narrow stripes, which wraps around so the edges meet. The strip then continues in a spiral, joined as you knit. It ends at the neckline with a fine I-cord edging.

SIZE
Small
If you want a larger top, work more stitches and more rows of wide stripes.

FINISHED MEASUREMENTS
Chest: 36 in / 91 cm
Total Length: on left side, 20½ in / 52 cm; on right side, 22 in / 56 cm

MATERIALS
Yarn: CYCA #2 (sport) Isager Tvinni (100% pure new Merino wool, 279 yd/255 m / 50 g)
Yarn Colors and Amounts:
Salmon 39s: 50 g
Gray-Pink 61s: 50 g
Ice Blue 10s: 50 g

Yarn: CYCA #0 (lace) Isager Silk Mohair (75% kid mohair, 25% mulberry silk, 232 yd/212 m / 25 g)
Yarn Colors and Amounts:
Blue 41: 25 g
Brick 28: 25 g
Yellow 59: 25 g

Needles: U. S. size 1.5 / 2.5 mm: 2 dpn (6 or 8 in / 15 or 20 cm) and 16 in / 40 cm circular U. S. size 2.5 / 3 mm: 1 dpn

Notions: 2 small buttons

GAUGE
25 sts and 56 rows/28 ridges in garter st with Tvinni on U. S. 1.5 / 2.5 mm needles = 4 x 4 in / 10 x 10 cm.
24 sts and 52 rows/26 ridges in garter st with Silk Mohair on U. S. 1.5 / 2.5 mm needles = 4 x 4 in / 10 x 10 cm.
1 strip is approx. 4 in / 10 cm wide
Adjust needle size to obtain correct gauge if necessary.

INSTRUCTIONS

The whole top is knitted on dpn U. S. 1.5 / 2.5 mm.
The circular needle is only used for the I-cord bind-off for finishing.

Technique
The pattern is based on School 1 (page 16), although the technique is different in that there are no intermediate stripes.

Diagram
The top is constructed with one long strip, knitted together in a spiral as you work. Just follow the numbers on the diagram on page 28 for the front and back of the top.

BACK AND FRONT
Knit one long strip as follows:

Front from 1 to 2: Follow the diagram, beginning at 1 for the front. The strip is knitted with 1 edge st on the right side and 2 on the left side, when the strip is seen from the RS.

1st wide stripe

With dpn U. S. 1.5 / 2.5 mm and Salmon, CO with 2 beg sts and then K-CO 24 sts (= 26 sts).

Row 1 (WS): P2, knit to last st, k1tbl.

Row 2 (RS): Sl 1 pwise, knit to end of row.

Row 3: Sl 2 pwise, knit to last st, p1.

Row 4: Sl 1 kwise, knit to end of row.

Rep Rows 3-4 until there are 47 rows/24 ridges on RS. The last row is on WS.

Color Changes on the Narrow Stripes

The last edge st before a color change is always purled.

Cross yarns **clockwise** when changing colors. Begin a RS row without a color change by crossing yarns **counter-clockwise**.

See also Changing Colors with Stripes on page 174.

*1st narrow stripe

Row 48 (RS): Sl 1 kwise, change to next color in sequence (here: Blue), knit to end of row.

Row 49 (WS): Sl 2 pwise, knit to last st, p1.

Row 50: Weave in blue end as you knit and, *at the same time*: Sl 1 kwise, knit to end of row.

Row 51: Sl 2 pwise, knit to last st, p1.

Row 52 (RS): Cross colors **counter-clockwise**, so Blue (the color you will knit with) is bought in towards you, under and back around Salmon (the color you won't use) and leave Blue on finger until you knit with it. Sl 1 kwise, knit to last st, p1.

Row 53 (WS): Sl 2 pwise, knit to last st, p1.

2nd narrow stripe

Knit with Salmon. Cross Salmon **clockwise** over Blue to be ready to knit with it.

Rows 54-59: Work as for Rows 48-53, but, on Row 56, cross Salmon **counter-clockwise** around Blue.

2nd wide stripe

Knit with Blue as for 1st wide stripe beginning on Row 2 This stripe should also have 24 ridges*.

Continue from * to *, following color sequence on diagram until reaching 2 on front.

Back from 3 to 4: Skip to 3 on back and continue to 4.

Front from 5 to 6: Skip to 5 on front and knit to S. The last row with Blue is on WS.

Now begin joining strip into a spiral. The whole strip should now measure 34-35½ in / 86-90 cm.

Continue, using 2 dpn.
Bend strip so corners meet and spiral can begin (see photo A). Insert needle tip into left corner of narrow Blue stripe (the side with 2 edge sts) and into right corner loop of wide Salmon stripe from below (from WS) and up on RS (see photo B).

Beginning where Blue yarn hangs, knit a wide stripe with Gray-Pink as follows:

Row 1 (RS): Sl 1 kwise, knit to last Blue st (photo C), p2tog with the Salmon corner loop and the last Blue st; turn.

Row 2 (WS): Insert the free needle from below and up in next/nearest Salmon edge st after/over corner loop, sl 1 kwise knit to last st, p1; turn.

Row 3: Sl 1 pwise, knit to last st, p2tog (= last st and edge st); turn.

Row 4: Insert the free needle from below and up in next edge st. Sl 1 kwise knit to last st, p1; turn.

Rep Rows 3-4 with 1 edge st each on right and left sides. The left is a joined st.

After a few rows have been joined, you should notice that the ridges are staggered as they meet, like teeth in a zipper (see photo D).

Color Changes: Always knit together directly **below** the next

DIAGRAM FOR SPIRAL TOP

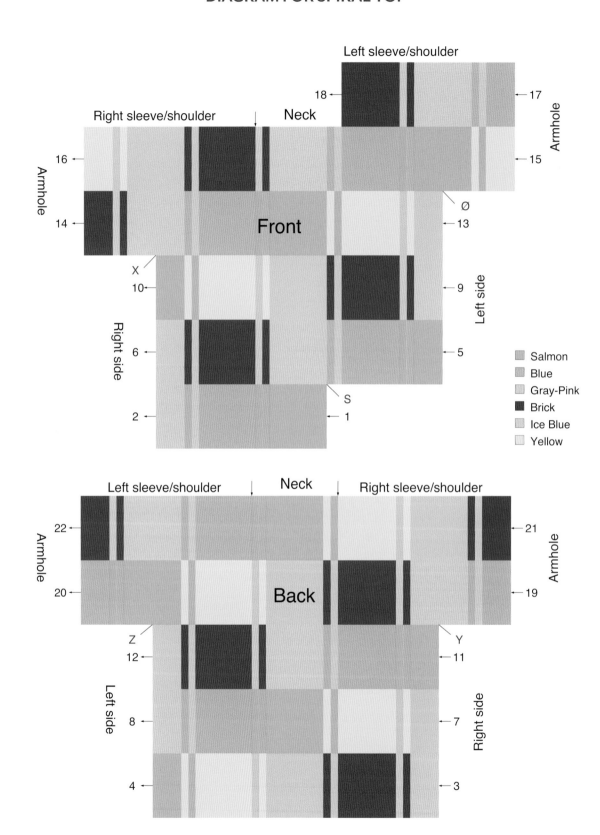

Left sleeve/shoulder

18 ← → 17

Armhole

Right sleeve/shoulder   Neck

16 ← → 15

Armhole   Ø

14 ←   Front   → 13

X
10 ←   9   Left side

Right side

6 ←   → 5

Salmon
Blue
Gray-Pink
Brick
Ice Blue
Yellow

S
2 ←   → 1

Left sleeve/shoulder   Neck   Right sleeve/shoulder

22 ←   → 21

Armhole   Back   Armhole

20 ←   → 19

Z   Y
12 ←   → 11

Left side   Right side

8 ←   → 7

4 ←   → 3

color. Just before a color change, the edge sts are very, very small, so here you have to be especially careful with where the needle is inserted into the join. You can enlarge the edge st with the needle tip and can maintain control if the stitch and ridge count coincide.

Continue following diagram to 6.

Back from 7 to 8: Skip to 7 and knit to 8.

Front from 9 to 10: Skip to 9 and knit to 10.

Back from 11 to 12: Skip to 11 and knit to 12.

Front from 13 to 14: Skip to 13 and knit to X (there are 12 ridges with gray-pink). Continue to 14 without joining and work 1 edge st at each side. Cut yarn and place sts on a holder for later.

Front from 15 to 16: With yellow, K-CO 26 sts (with 2 beg sts); do not tighten but leave space between the sts.
Knit without joining with 1 edge st at each side from 15 to 0 (there are 12 ridges with Salmon). Now knit together with 13, beginning at the center of the wide Ice Blue stripe and knit until reaching 16. Cut yarn and place sts on a holder for later.

Front from 17 to 18: With Blue, K-CO 26 sts (with 2 beg sts), leaving space between the sts. Now knit from 17, joining to 15; knit until reaching 18. Cut yarn and place sts on a holder for later.

Back from 19 to 20: With Blue, K-CO 26 sts (with 2 beg sts. Knit without joining with 1 edge st at each side from 19 to Y (there are 12 ridges with Gray-Pink). Now knit together with 11, continuing to Z (there are 12 ridges with Salmon). Continue to 20 without joining. Cut yarn and place sts on a holder for later.

Back from 21 to 22: With Brick, K-CO 26 sts (with 2 beg sts). Knit, joining to 19 until reaching 22.

FINISHING RIGHT SHOULDER AND ARMHOLE

Over right shoulder, knit a triangle to allow for a good fit. Turn with German short rows (DS, see page 186).

Triangle
With Ice Blue and U. S. 1.5 / 2.5 mm needle, pick up and knit 24 sts along wide Brick stripe of front right shoulder. Photo E shows the finished neck edge.
Row 1 (WS): Sl 1 pwise, knit to end of row.
Row 2 (RS): Sl 1 pwise, knit until 2 sts rem; turn.

Row 3: DS (= pull st until it flips and 2 legs are on needle—see page 186), knit to end of row.
Row 4: Sl 1 pwise, knit until 1 st before DS (here: k19); turn.
Rep Rows 3-4 until turning with 1 DS, k1.
Next Row (RS): Work 1 row over all 24 sts: Sl 1 pwise, *knit DS as one st, k1)*; rep from * to * to end of row.

Next Row: Sl 1 pwise, knit to end of row. Do not cut yarn.
Turn to WS of top.

Join triangle sts with Yellow edge sts on back right shoulder, and BO. Continue, joining remaining shoulder seam with Kitchener st.

Armhole Edge
Place held sts of 14 and 16 on circular, and, with Ice Blue, pick up and knit 52 sts over 21 and 19. Work I-cord BO as follows: K-CO 2 sts on left needle tip, where picking up and knitting finished (= 106 sts).
With circular in left hand and dpn U. S. 2.5 / 3 mm in right hand, work:
Row 1 (RS): K1, sl 1, k1, psso. Slide the 2 sts back onto circular. Rep Row 1.

Make sure the bind-off is not too tight. If necessary, use larger needles. Seam underarms with Kitchener st on RS.

FINISHING LEFT SHOULDER AND ARMHOLE

Seam left shoulder and sleeve seam at top with Kitchener st on RS, but leave the 24 ridges nearest neck as a slit.

Work I-cord BO along armhole as for right side.

NECK EDGING

Pick up and Knit: Place the 26 sts from 18 (on diagram) on a holder. Go to base of slit on left shoulder and, on RS with Ice Blue and circular, pick up and knit 24 sts along the wide Brick stripe. Knit the held 26 sts, pick up and knit 1 st in corner (between 18 and front neck), 36 sts along front neck, 1 st in corner (between front and triangle), 11 sts along triangle (1 st after each ridge), 60 sts along back neck and slit.

Place markers for buttonholes (loops): 1 marker at about center of slit and 1 at front by neck.

I-cord BO

Knit a narrow I-cord bind-off as on armholes and knit a button loop at each marker as follows: *K2, slip sts back to left needle*; rep from * to * a total of 4 times and continue as for button loop.

Sew buttons on back opposite button loops.

2
SQUARES

SQUARES

SCHOOL 2

Squares knitted together in a block pattern are called entrelac. In this school, they are used in a somewhat untraditional way. I suggest that you begin by reviewing School 1, if you haven't read through it already. The squares here are knitted up on the diagonal and purled down on the diagonal. The ridges of the purl squares will lean vertically in the finished piece, while the ridges of the knit squares will be horizontal. The squares can also be knitted together in other directions than those I've chosen. In that case, just place the stitches from each square on a holder until you join them later.

FINISHED MEASUREMENTS
Entire Swatch: 7½ x 7½ in / 19 x 19 cm
Single Square: slightly less than 1½ x 1½ in / 4 x 4 cm

MATERIALS
Yarn: CYCA #3 (DK, light worsted)
Filcolana Pernilla (100% pure new wool, 191 yd/175 m / 50 g)
Colors:
Nougat Heather 973 (gray-brown)
Isabella Heather 820 (pink)
Marzipan Heather 977 (natural white)
Willow Heather 822 (khaki)
Aqua Mist Heather 808 (turquoise)
Acacia Heather 825 (curry)
Dijon Heather 827 (red-brown)

Needles: U. S. size 2.5 / 3 mm: 2 dpn and 24 in / 60 cm circular

SWATCH
Diagram
The diagram shows the entire swatch. The numbers on the squares indicate the order of knitting.

Stitches and Ridges
One square can have any number of stitches. There should be the same number of stitches and ridges.
The pattern has 3 different sizes of squares: squares that are 10 sts and 10 ridges (swatch), squares that are 13 sts and 13 ridges (Checkerboard Vest), and squares that are 20 sts and 20 ridges (Reddish Pillow Cover). The swatch is constructed with 5 x 5 squares. Each square is 10 sts and 10 ridges.

PANEL 1
*This panel consists of one **purl square** with **vertical ridges**.*

SQUARE 1
The first square is on the lower left corner (photo A).
With gray-brown and dpn, K-CO 10 (13, 20) sts (with 2 beg sts). When comfortable, change to circular.
Row 1 (WS): *P10 (13, 20).*
Row 2 (RS): *Sl 1 kwise, p9 (12, 19).*
Row 3 (WS): *Sl 1 kwise, p9 (12, 19).*
Rep Rows 2-3 until there are 10 (13, 20) ridges on RS and 11 (14,

Entrelac

Entrelac is an old knitting technique; in Scandinavia, it's most often worked in Norway, Sweden, Finland, and Estonia, but not in Denmark. The Danish name for it, *neverkont*, comes from the Finnish people known as Savonians, who lived in North Sweden, very close to the Norwegian border, in the 1500s and 1600s. They were strongly encouraged to settle there by the Swedish king, who exempted them from taxes.

The Savonians used a type of backpack—a *kont*, made from woven birchbark that was called *never*. The knitting technique was named for its visual resemblance to that woven birchbark, even though it is knitted. Most often, entrelac is knitted with small stockinette squares, worked back and forth on the right side. But you can, as this school instructs, turn the work after every row, if you are using short double-pointed needles (6 in / 15 cm) or a circular needle.

DIAGRAM FOR SCHOOL 2

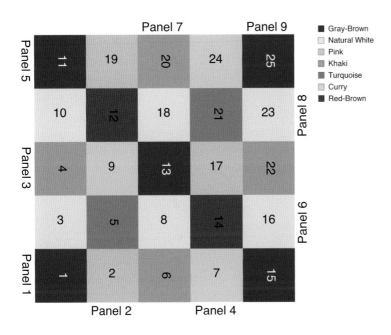

21) ridges on WS (photo A). The last row is on WS. Both working yarn and yarn end hang on right side of square.

Cut yarn, weave in end, and leave sts on needle.

PANEL 2

This panel consists of two **knit squares** with **horizontal ridges**. Direction of knitting: Bottom up, leaning to the left.

SQUARE 2

Holding Square 1 with RS facing you, with pink: K-CO 10 (13, 20) sts as an extension of sts on Square 1 (photo B).

Row 1 (RS): K9 (12, 19), p2tog = 10, (13, 20) sts; turn.
NOTE: Now 1 st of the 10 (13, 20) sts of Square 1 has been used up.
Row 2 (WS): Sl 1 kwise, knit to end of row; turn.
Row 3 (WS): Sl 1 pwise, k8 (11, 18), p2tog; turn.
Row 4: Sl 1 kwise, knit to end of row; turn.
Row 5: Sl 1 pwise, k8 (11, 18), p2tog (photo C); turn.
Rep Rows 4-5 until there are 10 (13, 20) ridges on RS and 11 (14, 21) ridges on WS (photo D).
Both yarn and yarn end hang on left side of square and all of the sts on Square 1 have been used up.
Cut yarn, weave in ends, and leave sts on needle.
Photo D shows Squares 1 and 2 on RS, and photo E shows the WS.

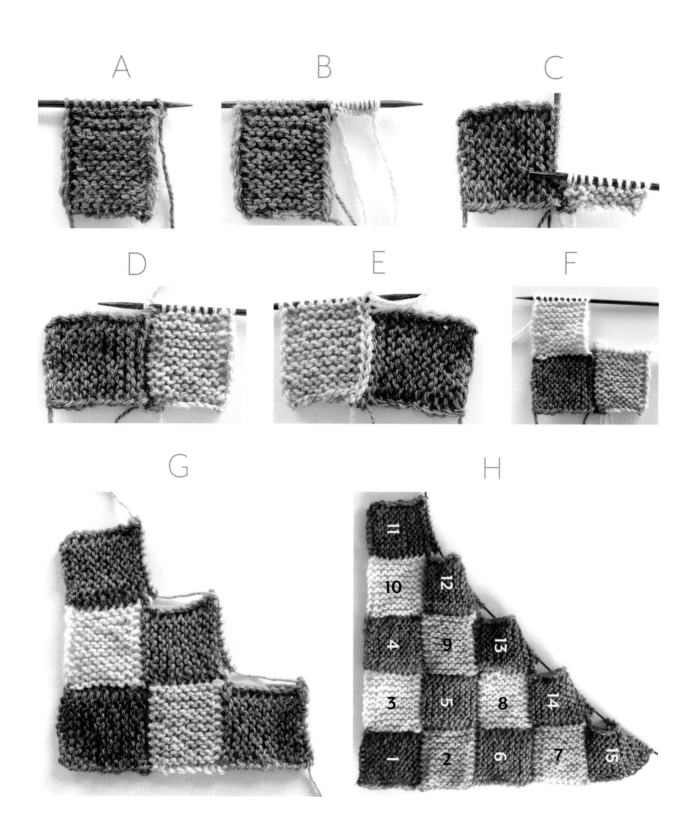

SQUARE 3

With RS facing you, using natural white, pick up and knit 12 (15, 22) sts (under both st loops) along square to left of square just knitted (here: Square 1): pick up and knit 1 st in every ridge, 1 st after last ridge and k1 in corner loop.

Row 1 (WS): Sl 1 pwise, k2tog, k6 (9, 16), k2tog, k1 [= 10, (13, 20) sts]; turn.

Row 2 (RS): Sl 1 pwise, k9 (12, 19); turn.

Row 3 (WS): Sl 1 pwise, k9 (12, 19); turn.

Rep Rows 2-3 until there are 10 (13, 20) ridges each on RS and WS. The last row is on RS (photo F). The yarn now hangs on left side. Cut yarn, fasten off, and leave sts on needle.

PANEL 3

*This panel consists of 3 **purl squares** with **vertical ridges**.*

Direction of knitting: Top down, leaning to the right.

SQUARE 4

This square is worked above the previously knitted square (here: Square 3).

Turn so WS faces you. With khaki, K-CO 10 (13, 20) sts as an extension of sts on row.

Row 1 (WS): P9 (12, 19), sl 1, k1, psso; turn.

Row 2 (RS): Sl 1 pwise, purl to end of row = 10 (13, 20) sts.

Row 3 (WS): Sl 1 kwise, P8 (13, 18), sl 1, k1, psso; turn.

Rep Rows 2-3 until there are 10 (13,

20) ridges on RS and 11 (14, 21) ridges on WS. The last row is on WS.
Cut yarn, weave in ends, and leave sts on needle.

SQUARE 5

Hold with WS facing you. With turquoise, pick up and purl 11 (14, 21) sts (see pages 184-185) along square below the one just worked (here: Square 3): pick up and purl 1 st in every ridge, 1 st after last ridge and move the last st to left needle with needle under yarn and k2tog.

Row 1 (RS): Sl 1 pwise, p7 (10, 17), p2tog, p1 = 10, (13, 20) sts; turn.

Row 2 (WS): Sl 1 kwise, p8 (11, 18), sl 1, k1, psso; turn.

Row 3 (RS): Sl 1 pwise, p9 (12, 19); turn.

Rep Rows 2-3 until there are 10 (13, 20) ridges each on RS and WS. The last row is on WS.

Cut yarn, weave in ends, and leave sts on needle.

SQUARE 6

Hold with WS facing you. With khaki, pick up and purl 12 (15, 22) sts along square to right of the one just worked (here: Square 2): pick up and purl 1 st in every ridge, and p1 in corner loop.

Row 1 (RS): Sl 1 kwise, p2tog, p6 (9, 16), p2tog, p1; turn.

Row 2 (WS): Sl 1 kwise, purl to end of row; turn.

Row 3 (RS): Sl 1 kwise, purl to end of row; turn.

Rep Rows 2-3 until there are 10 (13, 20) ridges each on RS and WS. The last row is on WS (photo G. The sts usually sit on a circular but here they

are on a yarn holder so they can be photographed flat).

Cut yarn, weave in ends, and leave sts on needle.

PANEL 4

This panel consists of 4 **knit squares** with **horizontal ridges**. Direction of knitting: Bottom up, leaning to the left.

SQUARE 7

Work as for Square 2, but with curry, to the right of the last worked square (here: Square 6).

SQUARE 8

With RS facing you, using natural white, pick up and knit 11 (14, 21) sts along square to left of last-worked square (here: Square 6): pick up 1 st in every ridge and 1 after last ridge; move last st to left needle and p2tog; turn.

Row 1 (WS): Sl 1 kwise, k7 (10, 17), k2tog, k1 = 10 (13, 20) sts; turn.

Row 2 (RS): Sl 1 pwise, k8 (11, 18), p2tog; turn.

Row 3 (WS): Sl 1 kwise, k9 (12, 19); turn.

Rep Rows 2-3 until there are 10 (13, 20) ridges each on RS and WS. The last row is on RS.

Cut yarn, weave in ends, and leave sts on needle.

SQUARE 9

Work as for Square 8, but with curry, along square to left (here: Square 5).

SQUARE 10

Work as for Square 3, but with natural white, above square to left of square just worked (here: Square 4).

PANEL 5

*This panel consists of 5 **purl squares** with **vertical ridges**. Direction of knitting: Top down, leaning to the right.*

SQUARE 11

Work as for Square 4, but with gray-brown, above last-worked square.

SQUARES 12, 13, AND 14

Work as for Square 5, but with red-brown, gray-brown, and red-brown (see diagram) between the respective squares.

SQUARE 15

Work as for Square 6, but with gray-brown, along next square. BO pwise on RS, when there are 9 (12, 19) ridges each on RS and WS after a WS row, but leave last st on needle (photo H).

From this point on, there are fewer and fewer squares in each panel, until at last there is only 1 square in upper right corner.

PANEL 6

This panel consists of 4 **knit squares** with **horizontal** ridges. Direction of knitting: Bottom up, leaning to the left.

SQUARE 16

Work as for Square 8, using natural white, over the last-worked square.
Pick up and knit 11 (14, 21) sts: k1 in end st from last-worked square (here: 15) and 1 st in every ridge, move last st to left needle and p2tog; turn.

SQUARES 17 AND 18

Work as for Square 8, using pink and natural white, above square to left of square just worked.

SQUARE 19

Work as for Square 8, using pink, over square to left of last-worked square.
BO 9 (12, 19) sts on WS when there are 9 (12, 19) ridges on both RS and WS; leave last st on needle, ready to begin next panel.

PANEL 7

*This panel consists of 3 **purl squares** with **vertical ridges**. Direction of knitting: Top down, leaning to the right.*

SQUARE 20

With WS facing you, using khaki, pick up and purl 11 (14, 21) sts along the last-worked square (here: 19): begin with p1 in end st of last-worked square, pick up 1 st in every ridge and 1 after last ridge.
Continue as for Square 11.

SQUARE 21

With turquoise, work as for Square 5 between two squares (here: 17 and 18).

SQUARE 22

With khaki, work as for Square 21 between two squares (here: 16 and 17) until there are 9 (12, 19) ridges on both RS and WS.
BO 9 (12, 19) sts purlwise on RS, leaving last st on needle.

PANEL 8

This panel consists of 2 **knit squares** with **horizontal** ridges. Direction of knitting: Bottom up, leaning to the left.

SQUARES 23 AND 24

Work, respectively, as for Square 16 with natural white, and as for Square 19 with curry, between 2 squares (here: Square 23 between 20 and 21 and Square 24 between 21 and 22).

PANEL 9

*This panel consists of 1 **purl square** with **vertical** ridges.*

SQUARE 25

Work with gray-brown, as for Square 22, between 2 squares (here: 23 and 24).
BO when there are 9 (12, 19) sts ridges on both RS and WS, after a WS row.

REDDISH PILLOW COVER

This pillow cover is worked as for the swatch in School 2, but some of the squares are striped, which makes the colors bloom. Knit an edging and sew on a backing for a very fine pillow cover.

FINISHED MEASUREMENTS
Cover: without edging, 15¾ x 15¾ in / 40 x 40 cm

MATERIALS
Yarn: CYCA #3 (DK, light worsted) Filcolana Pernilla (100% pure new wool, 191 yd/175 m / 50 g)
Yarn Colors and Amounts:
Merlot Heather 804 (burgundy): 50 g
Dijon Heather 827 (red-brown): 15 g
Isabella Heather 820 (rose): 15 g
Chrysanthemum Heather 810 (rust): 15 g
Cantaloupe Heather 826 (salmon): 15 g
Boysenberry Heather 807 (red-violet): 15 g
Acacia Heather 825 (curry): 15 g
Malve Heather 829 (pink): 15 g

Needles: U. S. size 2.5 / 3 mm: 2 dpn and 48 in / 120 cm circular U. S. size 2.5 / 3 mm: 1 dpn

Notions: insert pillow 15¾ x 15¾ in / 40 x 40 cm fleece for backing (www.stofogstil.dk): 16½ x 16½ / 42 x 42 cm

GAUGE
24 sts and 52 rows/26 ridges in garter st = 4 x 4 in / 10 x 10 cm.
1 square: 3¼ x 3¼ in / 8 x 8 cm.
Adjust needle size to obtain correct gauge if necessary.

INSTRUCTIONS
Begin with dpn and change to circular later.

Technique
The pattern is based on School 2 (page 34) with 3 sizes of squares. Learn the technique by working the first 3-4 panels of the swatch.

Diagram
1 little square = 1 st and 1 ridge/2 knit rows.

Stitches and Ridges
Each square has 20 sts and 20 ridges.

PILLOW COVER
Follow the diagram on page 42, which indicates the number of stitches and ridges, colors, and direction of knitting. Otherwise, follow the largest size in the pattern in School 2.

DIAGRAM FOR REDDISH PILLOW COVER

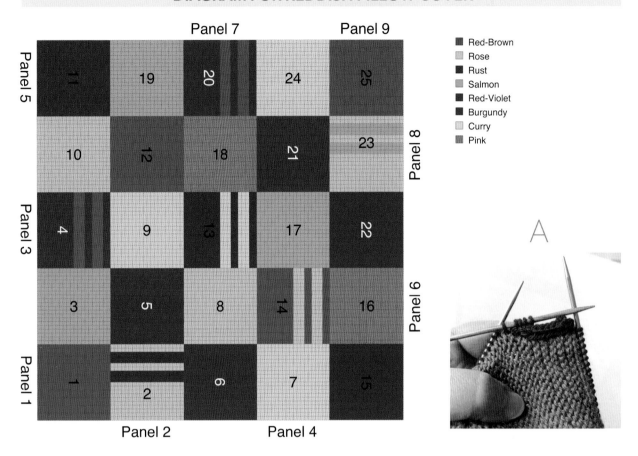

Panel 7   Panel 9

Panel 5

11	19	20	24	25
10	12	18	21	23
4	9	13	17	22
3	5	8	14	16
1 / 2	6	7	15

Panel 3

Panel 1

Panel 2   Panel 4

Panel 8

Panel 6

Color key:
- Red-Brown
- Rose
- Rust
- Salmon
- Red-Violet
- Burgundy
- Curry
- Pink

A

Colors and Stripes

The colors are worked as shown on diagram. Most squares are single-color, except for Squares 2, 4, 13, 14, 20, and 23, which are worked with stripes as follows:

Main color: 10 ridges
Stripe color: 3 ridges
Main color: 2 ridges
Stripe color: 3 ridges
Main color: 2 ridges

FINISHING
I-Cord Edging

Use long circular and 2 dpn as "helpers."

Work as for I-Cord Edging (see page 182) as follows:

Pick up and knit: Begin in one corner and, with burgundy, pick up and knit sts around cover: 20 sts along each square, K-CO 4 sts on left needle (where pick up and knit round began).
*Knit cord along one side, beginning on Row 2 (see photo A and page 182).
Knot on corner: Continue with cord for 2 in / 5 cm but do not join with cover, tie knot, and return sts to dpn*. Continue, repeating from

*to * until you've worked I-cord along each side with a knot at each corner.

Backing

Fold seam allowance to wrong side and stitch to cover inside edging, leaving enough open to insert pillow. Insert pillow and stitch rest of opening.

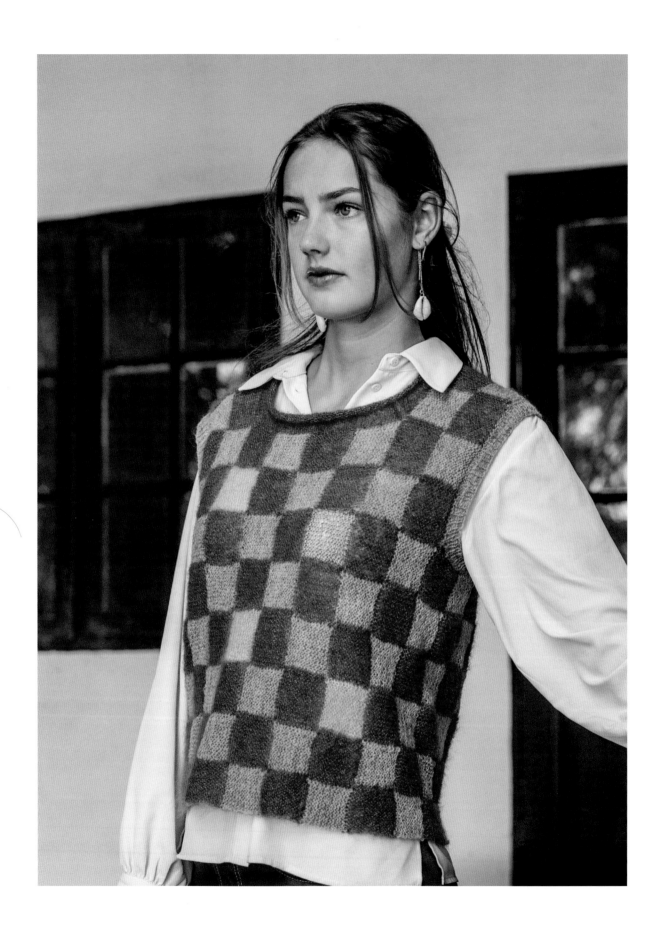

CHECKERBOARD VEST

This checkerboard vest is knitted alternately with mohair and Merino wool, for an especially luxurious look that dresses up the vest and you.

SIZE
Small/Medium

FINISHED MEASUREMENTS
Chest: 39½ in / 100 cm
Total Length: 19¾ in / 50 cm

MATERIALS
Yarn: CYCA #2 (sport) Isager Tvinni (100% pure new Merino wool, 279 yd/255 m / 50 g)
Yarn Colors and Amounts:
Salmon 39s: 100 g

Yarn: CYCA #0 (lace) Isager Silk Mohair (75% kid mohair, 25% mulberry silk, 232 yd/212 m / 25 g)
Yarn Colors and Amounts:
Brick 28: 50 g
Light Salmon 62: 25 g

Yarn: CYCA #0 (lace) Isager Japansk Bomuld (Japanese Cotton) (100% cotton, 344 yd/315 m / 50 g)
Yarn Colors and Amounts:
Peach 398: 50 g

Needles: U. S. size 1.5 / 2.5 mm: 2 dpn and 16 and 24 in / 40 and 60 cm circulars

GAUGE
25 sts and 56 rows/28 ridges in garter st with Tvinni on U. S. 1.5 / 2.5 mm needles = 4 x 4 in / 10 x 10 cm.
24 sts and 52 rows/26 ridges in garter st with Silk Mohair on U. S. 1.5 / 2.5 mm needles = 4 x 4 in / 10 x 10 cm.
4 joined squares = 4 x 4 in / 10 x 10 cm
Adjust needle size to obtain correct gauge if necessary.

INSTRUCTIONS
The whole vest is worked in one piece.

Technique
The pattern is based on School 2, page 34 and the diagram on page 47. Learn the technique by making the swatch. You can also just begin the vest and measure the gauge once you've worked at least 10 squares. Always end a square so the yarn is in position to knit the next square without cutting yarn.

Diagram
The diagram consists of squares, worked in numerical order.
All the brick squares are knitted.
All other squares are purled.

Stitches and Ridges
Each square has 13 sts and 13 ridges.

BACK AND FRONT

Follow the middle size for the pattern in School 2 and work the first 4 panels (Squares 1 to 10) as for School 2's first 4 panels, alternating Tvinni Salmon and Silk Mohair Brick.

Then work next panel as for Panel 3 of School 2 with colors on diagram, but longer.

Now you can measure the gauge: 1 square measures approx. 2 x 2 in / 5 x 5 cm and a block of 4 joined squares measures 4 x 4 in / 10x 10 cm.

Continue following diagram. From now on, we'll only mention those squares that vary from those in the school and have already been knitted.

Squares with **green** lines **21, 65, 84, 98, 102, 105, 149** (only top half), **161, 170, 173, and 176:** End by placing sts on a holder for later.

Square 22

Purl on WS. Begin with pick up and purl 1 into Square 21's outermost st and continue picking up and purling sts along side of 21.

Squares 69, 85, 105, 106, 162, and 171: Pick up and purl sts as for Square 22.

Squares 34 and 49: Work as for Square 4 in School 2.

Squares **67, 104, 148, and 175:** (at shoulders) Work as for Square 3 in School 2; BO on WS when there are 12 ridges on RS.

Square 68: Work as for Square 20 in School 2, but end by placing sts on a holder when there are 13 ridges on RS and 12 ridges on WS.

Squares 140, 155, and 166: (on right side of back at side seam) BO after 13 ridges on RS.

Squares 161 and 170: (at back neck) Place sts on a holder after 8 ridges + 1 row on WS.

Squares 162 and 171: Should have 8 sts and 13 ridges.

FINISHING

Sew right side seam. It sits slightly to the back.
Join both shoulder seams.

NECKBAND

Work with Silk Mohair Brick and U.S. 1.5 / 2.5 mm, 24 in / 60 cm circular.

Rnd 1, pick up and knit:

Place all held sts for front and back necks on circular, pm at each corner. Pick up and knit 6 sts along Square 175, 1 st in corner 13 sts along Square 171, k13 from 170, puk 13 sts along 162, k13 of 161, 1 st in corner, k6 of 149, puk 13 sts along 104 and 101, 1 st in corner, puk 13 sts along 85, k13 of 84, puk

13 sts along 69, k13 of 65, puk 1 st in corner, 13 sts of 66 and 13 sts along 68 (= 172 sts total).

Rnd 2: Knit 1 rnd, decreasing st count to 12 sts along each whole square (= 160) sts.

Rnd 3: Knit, and, in each corner, k2tog k1 (corner st), sl 1, k1, psso (see page 172). There are now 8 fewer sts.

Rnd 4: Knit.

Rep Rnds 3-4 another 2 times for a total of 8 rnds.

Now knit 8 rnds without further decreasing. BO loosely.

ARMHOLE EDGINGS

Work with Tvinni Salmon and U.S. 1.5 / 2.5 mm 16 in / 40 cm circular.

Right Side

Rnd 1, pick up and knit:

Beginning at base of armhole, pick up and knit sts as for neck with 12 sts along each square and 1 st in each corner.

Rnd 2: Purl, and *at the same time* p2tog in each corner (= decrease 1 st before and 1 st after each corner).

Rnd 3: Knit, decreasing so there will be 11 sts along each square, including the 2 corner sts.

Now work 7 rnds k1, p1 ribbing. BO in ribbing.

Left Side

Work as for right side.

DIAGRAM FOR CHECKERBOARD VEST

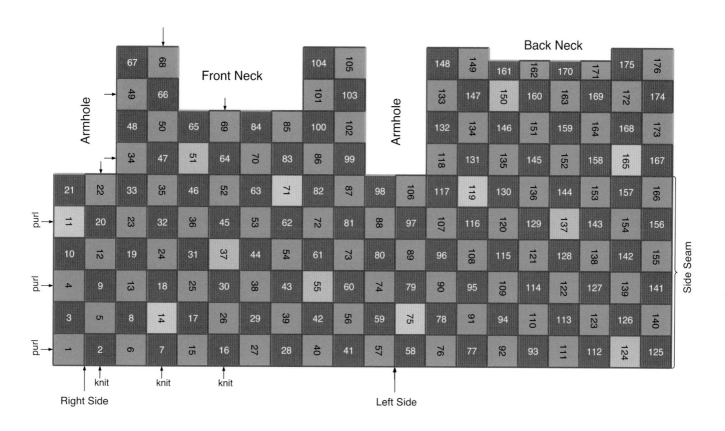

Silk Mohair Brick
Tvinni Salmon
Japanese Bomuld Perch
Silk Mohair Light Salmon

Black numbers: Squares with black numbers are **purled** leaning down to the right.

White numbers: Squares with white numbers are **knitted** leaning up to the left.

Finishes with green lines: Place sts on a holder for later.

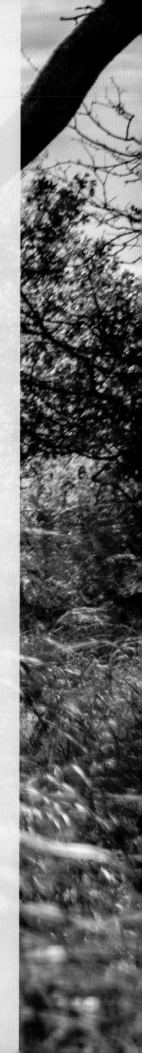

3

TRI-SQUARES

TRI-SQUARES

SCHOOL 3

At first glance, these tri-squares look like domino-knit squares, but they are completely different. A "tri-square" is a triangle knitted from the bottom up with short rows and wrapped stitches. Another triangle is knitted from the top down alongside the first, so, and together they form a square. The squares are crocheted together.

FINISHED MEASUREMENTS
Whole Swatch: 9¾ x 9¾ in / 25 x 25 cm
Single Triangle: approx. 3¼ x 3¼ in / 8.5 x 8.5 cm

MATERIALS
Yarn: CYCA #3 (DK, light worsted) Filcolana Pernilla (100% pure new wool, 191 yd/175 m / 50 g)
Yarn Colors and Amounts:
Nougat Heather 973 (gray-brown)
Oatmeal Heather 978 (gray-beige)
Marzipan Heather 977 (natural white)
Parrot Green Heather 824 (green)
Aqua Mist Heather 808 (turquoise)
Cantaloupe Heather 826 (salmon)
Acacia Heather 825 (curry)

Needles: U. S. size 2.5 / 3 mm: 2 dpn
Crochet Hook: U. S. size D-3 / 3 mm

SWATCH
This swatch consists of triangles in 9 different color combinations. These are crocheted together for finishing. Step-by-step photos show how to work the center triangle.

ONE TRI-SQUARE
Triangle 1
This triangle is the first half of Tri-Square 1.
With gray-brown and U. S. 2.5 / 3 mm needles, K-CO 20 sts (with 2 beg sts).
Row 1 (WS): Knit to last st, p1 turn.
Row 2 (RS), forward: Sl 1 kwise, knit to last st, weaving in yarn end as you knit. Sl 1 pwise (see 1 wrapped st, before turning); turn.
Row 3 (WS), return: Sl 1 pwise (see 1 wrapped st, after turning). You've now wrapped around 1 st (from now on called 1 wrapped st). Knit to end of row (1 wrapped st + 19 sts); turn.
Row 4, forward: Sl 1 pwise, knit to last st before wrapped st (a total of 18 sts), sl 1 pwise; turn.
Row 5, return: Work as for Row 3 (2 wrapped sts + 18 sts); turn.
Row 6, forward: Sl 1 pwise, knit until 1 st before last wrapped st (a total of 17 sts), sl 1 pwise; turn.
Row 7, return: Work as for Row 3 (3 wrapped sts + 17 sts).
Row 8, forward: Sl 1 pwise, knit until 1 st before last wrapped st (a total of 16 sts), sl 1 pwise; turn.
Row 9, return: Work as for Row 3 (4 wrapped sts + 16 sts).
Continue as est until there are 18 wrapped sts + 2 sts after a return row on WS.

Next Row (RS), forward: Sl 1 pwise, sl 1 pwise; turn.

Next Row (WS), return: Sl 1 pwise, k1; turn.

Next Row: Sl 1 pwise, take yarn back over, between the 2 needles, and place wrap over on left needle, so the last st is also wrapped (20 wraps, photo A).

Cut yarn and weave in ends, leaving sts on needle.

Triangle 2

This triangle is the second half of the first square. It completes the square.

Work with salmon.

Row 1 (RS): K1tbl, 1 uplink (see below); turn.

Row 2 (WS): K2; turn.

Row 3: Sl 1 pwise, k1, 1 uplink; turn.

Row 4: K3; turn.

Row 5: Sl 1 pwise, k2, 1 uplink; turn.

Row 6: Knit to end of row; turn.

Row 7: Sl 1 pwise, knit until you meet the next gray-brown st, 1 uplink; turn.

Rep Rows 6-7 with more and more salmon sts until only 1 gray-brown st rem after a WS row/return row. On photo B, you can see 6 salmon sts and 14 gray-brown sts.

NOTE: The total number of sts is always 20.

When all the wraps have been used, end with knit 1 row on WS. The tri-square is now finished (photo C).

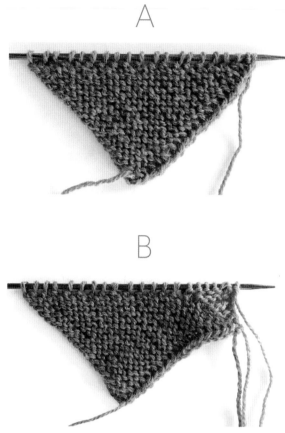

A

B

C

Wrapped stitch (wr st)

A wrapped stitch is a stitch that has been wrapped by the working yarn.

1 wrapped st before turning: End with sl 1 pwise (= insert the right needle into a stitch as if to purl), with yarn held over needle, before slipping stitch unworked under the yarn. Turn work.

1 wrapped st after turning (next row): Sl 1 pwise (= insert the right needle into a stitch, with yarn held below needle, slip st and continue working. Now the yarn is wrapped on the left around the stitch.

Uplink

When, on next row, you come to a wrapped st, work as follows:

1 uplink: Insert needle into wrap around stitch and lift it unworked onto right needle; knit stitch, and draw wrap over stitch.

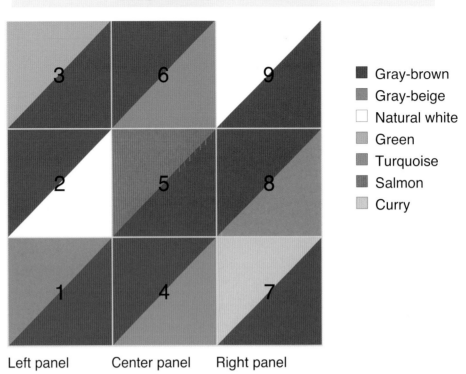

Left panel   Center panel   Right panel

Gray-brown
Gray-beige
Natural white
Green
Turquoise
Salmon
Curry

Cut yarn and place rem sts on a holder for later.

The already-worked tri-square is the center, Tri-Square 5. The 9 tri-squares are worked the same way, with these colors:

1: Gray-brown and gray-beige. End by binding off.
2: Natural white and gray-brown. End by binding off.
3: Gray-brown and green. End by binding off.
4: Turquoise and gray-brown.
5: Gray-brown and salmon.
6: Turquoise and gray-brown.
7: Gray-brown and curry.

8: Gray-beige and gray-brown.
9: Gray-brown and natural white.

JOINING
The 9 tri-squares are crocheted together with gray-beige and hook U. S. D-3 / 3 mm (see Joining with Crochet on page 185). Arrange the tri-squares as shown in picture of swatch.

Left Panel
Tri-Squares 1 and 2: Fold Tri-Square 2 down over Tri-Square 1 with RS facing RS, so Tri-Square 2's natural white cast-on loops lie parallel with the gray-beige edge sts of Tri-Square 1. Crochet them

together with slip sts so each cast-on loop of Tri-Square 2 is joined with an edge st of Tri-Square 1. Turn Tri-Square 2 back as before.
Tri-Squares 2 and 3: Likewise fold Tri-Square 3 down over Tri-Square 2 with right sides facing, so Tri-Square 3's gray-brown cast-on loops lie parallel with Tri-Square 2's gray-brown edge sts. Crochet them together. Turn Tri-Square 3 back as before.

Center Panel
Crochet Tri-Squares 4, 5, and 6 together the same way; the colors are different. Turn each back.

Right Panel

Crochet Tri-squares 7, 8, and 9 together the same way; the colors are different. Turn each back.

Crocheting Panels Together

Slip held sts of center panel onto a needle. Hold the panel with stitches on the needle with right sides facing and parallel to left panel, so left panel's edge sts lie nearest you and the needle with sts is furthest back. Work 1 slip st through 1 edge st of left panel and 1 st on needle. Put panels aside.

Crochet the middle and right panels together the same way.

Knitting Tip

Check regularly to make sure the stitch count is correct. Count the stitches on the needle after a WS row. Also count the number of ridges on the right side and add these 2 numbers together. The total should always be the same as the number of stitches cast on for a square.

VIKING COAT

Here's a special coat constructed with 6 tri-squares. The coat is reversible. One side goes up to the armholes with horizontal garter ridges, while the other side points up vertically.

SIZE
One size

FINISHED MEASUREMENTS
Chest: 47¼-63 in / 120-160 cm
Total Length: approx. 31½ in / 80 cm

MATERIALS
Yarn: CYCA #3 (DK, light worsted) Filcolana Pernilla (100% pure new wool, 191 yd/175 m / 50 g)
Yarn Colors and Amounts:
Charcoal 956: 300 g
Chrysanthemum Heather 810 (rust): 150 g
Acacia Heather 825 (curry): 150 g
You'll need slightly less than 1 ball of yarn for each of triangles of the coat.
Needles: U. S. size 2.5 / 3 mm: 1 dpn (6 or 8 in / 15 or 20 cm long) and 24 in / 60 cm circular

GAUGE
25 sts and 52 rows/26 ridges in garter st = 4 x 4 in / 10 x 10 cm.
1 tri-square = approx. 15¾ x 15¾ in / 40 x 40 cm
Adjust needle size to obtain correct gauge if necessary.

INSTRUCTIONS
Technique
The pattern is based on School 3 (page 50) and the diagram on page 56. Learn the technique by knitting the entire sample swatch or only one tri-square.

Diagram
The diagram consists of 6 large tri-squares, each knitted with 2 triangles. The colors are shown on the diagram. The lines show the direction of the ridges and the arrows indicate the direction of knitting.

TRI-SQUARE 1
Triangle 1
This triangle is the first half of Tri-Square 1.
With curry and circular, K-CO 100 sts (with 2 beg sts).
Row 1 (WS): Knit to last st, p1; turn.
Row 2 (RS): Sl 1 kwise, knit to last st, weaving in yarn end. Sl 1 pwise (see 1 wrapped st before turning, on page 55); turn.

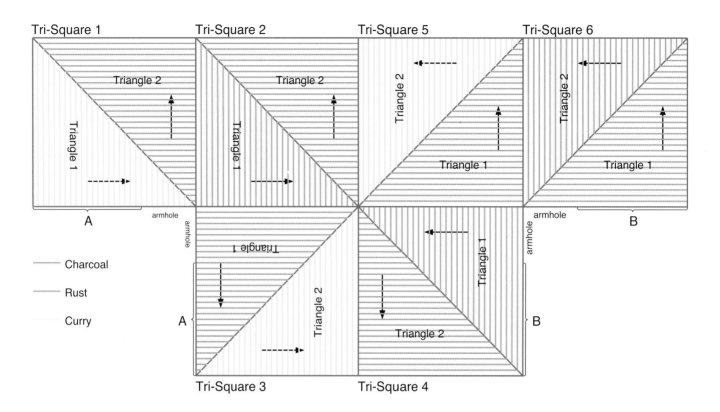

Row 3 (WS), return: Sl 1 pwise (see wrapped st, after turning, page 51). There is now 1 wrapped st, abbreviated going forward as "1 wr st"; knit to end of row (= 1 wr st + 99 sts). Turn.

Row 4, forward: Sl 1 pwise, knit until 1 st before wr st (= a total of 98 sts), sl 1 pwise; turn.

Row 5, return: Work as for Row 3 (2 wr sts + 98 sts); turn.

Row 6, forward: Sl 1 pwise, knit until 1 st before last wr st (= a total of 97 sts), sl 1 pwise; turn.

Row 7, return: Work as for Row 3 (3 wr sts + 97 sts); turn.

Row 8, forward: Sl 1 pwise, knit until 1 st before last wr st (= a total of 96 sts), sl 1 pwise; turn.

Row 9, return: Work as for Row 3 (4 wr sts + 96 sts).

Continue the same way until there are 98 wrapped sts + 2 sts after a return row on WS.

Next Row (RS), forward: Sl 1 pwise, sl 1 pwise; turn.

Next Row (RS), return: Sl 1 pwise, k1; turn.

Next Row: Sl 1 pwise, take yarn back over between the 2 needles and place the wr st over left needle, so the last st is also wrapped. Do not cut yarn but leave yarn hanging at the side for later.

Triangle 2

This triangle is the second half of Tri-Square 1. It completes the square.

Knit with charcoal.

Row 1 (RS): K1tbl, 1 uplink (see School 3); turn.

Row 2 (WS): K2; turn.

Row 3: Sl 1 pwise, k1, 1 uplink; turn.

Row 4: K3; turn.

Row 5: Sl 1 pwise, k2, 1 uplink; turn.
Row 6: Knit across; turn.
Row 7: Sl 1 pwise, knit to next curry st, 1 uplink; turn.

Rep Rows 6-7 with more and more charcoal sts, until 1 curry st rem after a WS/return row.
When all wr sts have been worked, end with knit 1 row on WS. The tri-square is now finished.
Cut yarn and place sts on a holder for later.

TRI-SQUARES 2 AND 4
Work as for Tri-Square 1 but with rust and charcoal.

TRI-SQUARES 3 AND 5
Work as for Tri-Square 1 but with charcoal and curry.

TRI-SQUARE 6
Work as for Tri-Square 1 but with charcoal and rust.

FINISHING
CROCHETING TOGETHER
Crochet the 6 tri-squares together with charcoal and hook U.S. D-3 /3 mm (see Joining, page 185).

Arrange the tri-squares as shown on diagram.

Tri-Squares 1 and 2
Fold Tri-Square 1 over Tri-Square 2 with right sides facing, so edge sts on Tri-Square 1's Triangle 2 lie parallel with cast-on loops of Tri-Square 2's Triangle 1. Crochet them together with the corresponding cast-on loops of Tri-Square 2. Begin and end in a corner. Set aside tri-squares.

Tri-Squares 5 and 6
Place sts of Tri-Square 6's Triangle 2 on circular needle and turn tri-square back. Fold Tri-Square 5 in over Tri-Square 6 with right sides facing, so edge sts on Tri-Square 5's Triangle 1 lie parallel with sts on Tri-Square 6's Triangle 2. Crochet edge sts and live sts together. Begin and end in a corner. Set tri-squares aside.

Tri-Squares 2 and 5
Place sts of Tri-Square 5's Triangle 2 on circular needle and fold tri-square back. Fold Tri-Squares 1 and 2 over Tri-Squares 5 and 6 with right sides facing, so edge sts on Tri-Square 2's Triangle 2 lie parallel with sts on Tri-Square 5's Triangle 2. Crochet edge sts together. Begin and end in a corner. Set tri-squares aside.

Tri-Squares 3 and 4
Place sts of Tri-Square 3's Triangle 2 on circular needle. Fold Tri-Square 3 in over Tri-Square 4 with right sides facing, so sts of Tri-Square 3's Triangle 2 lie parallel with edge sts on Tri-Square 4's Triangle 2. Crochet together. Set tri-squares aside.

Tri-Squares 3 and 4 Joined to Tri-Squares 2 and 5
Fold top row of tri-squares down over Tri-Squares 3 and 4 with right sides facing, so Tri-Squares 2 and 5 cover Tri-Squares 3 and 4. Crochet cast-on loops from Tri-Square 5's Triangle 1 together with edge sts of Tri-Square 4's Triangle 1 and then through edge sts from Tri-Square 2's Triangle 1 and cast-on loops of Tri-Square 3's Triangle 1.

LEFT ARMHOLE EDGE AND SIDE SEAM
Armhole Edge Along Tri-Square 3
Work as for Garter Stitch Edging with 2 Edge Stitches, page 181.
Use U.S. 2 .5 / 3 mm, 24 in / 60 cm circular and after 1st row a dpn U.S. 2 .5 / 3 mm to help.

Ridges
Row 1 (RS), pick up and knit:
Beginning at corner between Tri-Squares 1 and 3, with charcoal, pick up and knit 48 sts along Tri-Square 3's triangle 1; turn.
Row 2 (WS): k2-in-1, k46, k2-in-1 (= 50 sts).

Garter Stitch Edging with 2 Edge Stitches
K-CO 7 sts as an extension of last row's sts and work along the 48 sts.
Row 1 (RS): Sl 2 pwise, k4, p2tog; turn.
Row 2 (WS): Sl 1 kwise, knit to end of row.
Rep Rows 1-2 until just before corner st; cut yarn.

Joining Left Side
Fold Tri-Squares 1 and 3 together with right sides facing, so sides A

and A are joined. With charcoal, crochet together until you reach armhole edge.

Armhole Edge Along Tri-Square 1

Change to circular U. S. 2.5 / 3 mm and curry and knit an edging along Tri-Square 1 corresponding to that on Tri-Square 3.

Sew edging together along the 7 rem sts.

RIGHT ARMHOLE EDGE AND SIDE SEAM
Armhole Edge Along Tri-Square 6

Beginning in corner, with charcoal, knit an edging along Tri-Square 6's triangle 1 as for Tri-Square 3.

Joining Right Side

Crochet seam as for left side.

Armhole Edge Along Tri-Square 4

Change to circular U. S. 2.5 / 3 mm and salmon and knit an edging along Tri-Square 4 corresponding to that on Tri-Square 1.

Sew edging together along the 7 rem sts.

BOXES PILLOW COVER

*16 tri-squares that look like small boxes are knitted one at a time and crocheted together in finishing.
Knit an edging around the cover, sew on the backing, and a new pillow is ready for the sofa.*

FINISHED MEASUREMENTS
without edging, 15 x 15 in / 38 x 38 cm

MATERIALS
Yarn: CYCA #3 (DK, light worsted) Filcolana Pernilla (100% pure new wool, 191 yd/175 m / 50 g)

Yarn Colors and Amounts:
Black 102 (black): 50 g
Medium Gray Heather 955 (gray): 50 g
Cantaloupe Heather 826 (salmon): 50 g
Acacia Heather 825 (curry): 50 g

Needles: U. S. size 2.5 / 3 mm: 2 dpn and 48 in / 120 cm circular
Crochet Hook: U. S. size D-3 / 3 mm

Notions: Insert pillow, 15 x 15 in / 38 x 38 cm, fleece fabric for backing (www.stofogstil.dk), 15 x 15 in / 38 x 38 cm

GAUGE
24 sts and 52 rows/26 ridges in garter st = 4 x 4 in / 10 x 10 cm.
1 tri-square = 3¾ x 3¾ in / 9.5 x 9.5 cm
Adjust needle size to obtain correct gauge if necessary.

INSTRUCTIONS
Technique
The pattern is based on School 3 (page 50) and the diagram on page 63.

Rule of Thumb
Always end on a row with p1 (edge st), when changing colors and, when applicable, weaving in ends. Change colors inside edge stitch.

TRI-SQUARE 1
Triangle 1
This triangle is the first half of Tri-Square 1.
With gray and dpn, K-CO 22 sts (with 2 beg sts).
Row 1 (WS): Knit to last st, p1; turn.
Row 2 (RS), forward: Sl 1 kwise, knit to last st, weaving in yarn end. Sl 1 pwise (see 1 wrapped st before turning, on page 51); turn.
Row 3 (WS), return: Sl 1 pwise (see 1 wrapped st after turning, page 51).
There is now 1 wrapped st, subsequently abbreviated as 1 wr st; knit to end of row (= 1 wr st + 21 sts). Turn.

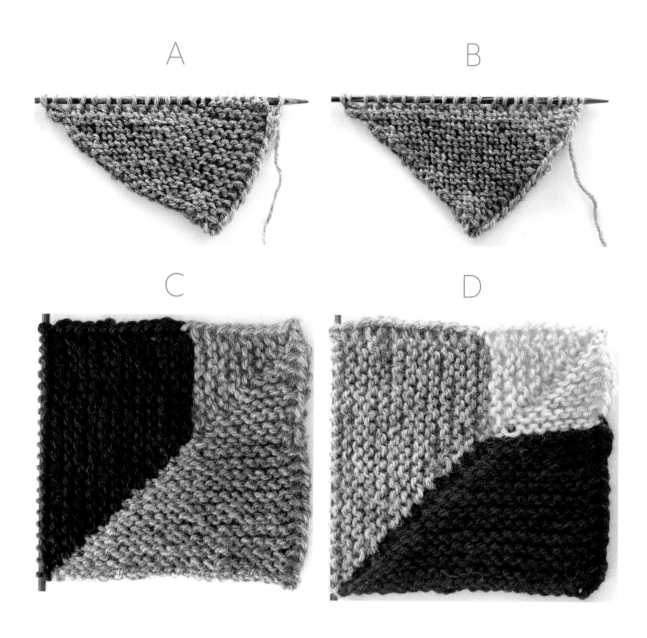

A

B

C

D

Row 4, forward: Sl 1 pwise, knit until 1 st before wr st (= a total of 20 sts), sl 1 pwise; turn.

Row 5, return: Work as for Row 3 (2 wr sts + 20 sts); turn.

Row 6, forward: Sl 1 pwise, knit until 1 st before last wr st (= 3 wr sts + 19 sts), sl 1 pwise; turn.

Row 7, return: Work as for Row 3.

Row 8, forward: Sl 1 pwise, knit until 1 st before last wr st (= 4 wr sts + 17 sts), sl 1 pwise; turn.

Row 9, return: Work as for Row 3.

Continue the same way until there are **13 wr sts** + 9 sts after a return row on WS, and **13 ridges** on RS (photo A). Cut gray, change to salmon, and continue as est until there are **20 wr sts + 2 sts**.

Next Row (RS), forward: Sl 1 pwise, sl 1 pwise; turn.

Next Row (RS), return: Sl 1 pwise, k1; turn.

Next Row: Sl 1 pwise, take yarn back over between the 2 needles and place the wr st over left needle, so the last st is also wrapped (photo B). Do not cut yarn but leave yarn hanging at the side for later.

■ Black
■ Gray
■ Salmon
■ Curry

Triangle 2

This triangle is the second half of Tri-Square 1. It completes the square.

Knit with charcoal.

Row 1 (RS): K1tbl, 1 uplink (see page 51); turn.

Row 2 (WS): K2; turn.

Row 3: Sl 1 pwise, k1, 1 uplink; turn.

Row 4: K3; turn.

Row 5: Sl 1 pwise, k2, 1 uplink; turn.

Row 6: Knit across; turn.

Row 7: Sl 1 pwise, knit until all salmon sts have been worked, 1 uplink; turn.

There are now **13 gray wr sts + 9 salmon sts**.

Change to black and rep Rows 6-7 with more and more black sts, until 1 gray st rem after a WS/return row.

When all the wr sts have been worked, end with knit 1 row on WS (photo C).

Cut yarn and place sts on a holder for later.

Knit a total of 8 of these tri-squares.

TRI-SQUARE 2

Work this tri-square as for Tri-Square 1, but begin with black and use curry as the contrast color. Finish with gray (photo D).

Knit a total of 8 of these tri-squares.

FINISHING

CROCHETING TOGETHER

Arrange tri-squares as on diagram; the text refers to the numbered squares. Crochet the 16 tri-squares together with hook U.S. D-3 / 3 mm (see Joining, page 185). Where two squares adjoin, use black.

PANEL 1

Tri-Squares 1 and 2: Fold Tri-Square 2 down over Tri-Square 1 with right sides facing, so cast-on loops of Tri-Square 2 are parallel to edge sts on Tri-Square 1. Crochet them together with slip sts through 1 cast-on loop and 1 edge st. Arrange tri-squares as before.

Tri-Squares 2 and 3: Fold Tri-Square 3 down over Tri-Square 2 with right sides facing, so cast-on loops of Tri-Square 3 are parallel to edge sts on Tri-Square 2.

Crochet them together with slip sts through 1 cast-on loop and 1 edge st. Arrange Tri-Square 3 as before.

Tri-Squares 3 and 4: Fold Tri-Square 4 down over Tri-Square 3 with right sides facing, so cast-on loops of Tri-Square 4 are parallel to edge sts on Tri-Square 3. Crochet them together with slip sts through 1 cast-on loop and 1 edge st. Set panel aside.

Panels 2, 3, and 4
Following diagram, crochet tri-squares together as est.

Joining panels
Arrange panels as on diagram.

Panels 1 and 2: Slip held sts of Panel 2 onto needle. Fold Panel 2 over Panel 1 with right sides facing, and crochet sts along Panel 2 together with edge sts of Panel 1's right side.

Panels 2 and 3: Slip held sts of Panel 3 onto needle. Fold Panel 3 over Panel 2 with right sides facing, and crochet sts along Panel 3 together with edge sts of Panel 2's right side.

Panels 3 and 4: Slip held sts of Panel 4 onto needle. Fold Panel 4 over Panel 3 with right sides facing, and crochet sts along Panel 4 together with edge sts of Panel 3's right side.

EDGING
Work as for Garter Stitch Edging with 2 Edge Stitches on page 181:

Ridge
Rnd 1, pick up and knit:
Slip the 88 sts along Panel 1 onto long circular and, with salmon, k88, *k1 in corner, pick up and knit 88 sts along next side (= 22 sts per tri-square)*; rep from * to * 2 more times.
Rnd 2: Purl 1 rnd.

Garter Stitch Edging with 2 Edge Stitches
Change to black and K-CO 7 sts on left needle (where picking up and knitting rnd began), work Garter Stitch Edging with 2 Edge Stitches. Join ends with Kitchener st.

BACKING
Turn seam allowance to wrong side and stitch to pillow cover inside edge sts, leaving enough space to insert pillow. Insert pillow and then close backing.

4
RIGHT ANGLES

RIGHT ANGLES

SCHOOL 4

Stripes (School 1) and Squares (School 2) are the foundations for this school, but if you're brave, you can skip both and begin here. Knit a corner square first, then a right angle along 2 sides of the square. Another, larger right angle is knitted around this block, and so on. If you continue adding right angles, you will end up with wonderful large squares. Use 4 squares (as on the swatch) for a pillow cover (see page 74), or continue adding right angles to one square for a larger square to fit the pillow.

FINISHED MEASUREMENTS
Whole Swatch: 8 x 8 in / 20 x 20 cm
Width of Leg of Right Angle:
approx. 1½ in / 4 cm

MATERIALS
Yarn: CYCA #3 (DK, light worsted)
Filcolana Pernilla (100% pure new wool, 191 yd/175 m / 50 g)
Yarn Colors and Amounts:
Acacia Heather 825 (curry)
Charcoal Heather 956 (charcoal)
Medium Gray 955 (dark gray)
Light Gray Heather 954 (medium gray)
Very Light Gray Heather 957 (light gray)

Needles: U. S. size 2.5 / 3 mm: dpn and 24 in / 60 cm circular

SWATCH
Knit a corner square and then surround it with larger and larger right angles, first Leg 1 and then Leg 2.

Stitches and Ridges
The number of stitches and ridges are optional, but the number of ridges should be the same as the number of stitches along the side where stitches were picked up. Here, Leg 1 has 10 stitches and more and more ridges in height.

CORNER SQUARE
Purl with curry; square consists of 10 sts and 10 ridges.
With curry and dpn, K-CO 10 sts (with 2 beg sts).
Row 1 (RS): Purl across.
Row 2 (WS): Sl 1 kwise, purl to

end of row.
Row 3 (RS): Sl 1 kwise, purl to end of row.
Rep Rows 2-3 until there are 10 ridges on both RS and WS after a WS row (photo A).
The yarn end hangs at lower left and working yarn is at top right corner. Cut yarn.

RIGHT ANGLE 1
Leg 1
Knit with charcoal; square consists of 10 sts and 10 ridges.
With charcoal and dpn, K-CO 10 sts as extension of corner square's 10 sts on needle (photo B).
Row 1 (RS): K9, p2tog (= 10 sts); turn.
Row 2 (WS): Sl 1 kwise, knit to end of row; turn.
Row 3 (RS): Sl 1 pwise, k8, p2tog; turn.

A   B   C

D   E

F   G

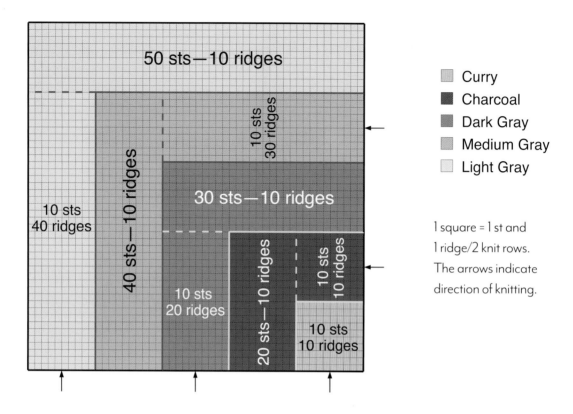

Curry
Charcoal
Dark Gray
Medium Gray
Light Gray

50 sts—10 ridges

10 sts
30 ridges

10 sts
40 ridges

40 sts—10 ridges

30 sts—10 ridges

10 sts
20 ridges

20 sts—10 ridges

10 sts
10 ridges

10 sts
10 ridges

1 square = 1 st and
1 ridge/2 knit rows.
The arrows indicate
direction of knitting.

Rep Rows 2-3 until there are 10 ridges on both RS and WS. The last row is on WS.
The working yarn is at right side (photo C).

Leg 2

Continue from Leg 1. The leg consists of 20 sts and 10 ridges.
Row 1 (RS), pick up and knit: Sl 1 pwise, k9, continue pick up and knit 11 sts over corner square's side: 1 st **before** every ridge, 1 st after last ridge in corner (= 21 sts); turn.
Row 2 (WS): Sl 1 pwise, k10, p2tog, knit to end of row (= 20 sts); turn.
Row 3: Sl 1 pwise, knit to end of row; turn.

Row 4: Sl 1 pwise, knit to end of row; turn.
Rep Rows 3-4 until Leg 2 has 10 ridges on both RS and WS (photo D). The last row is on RS and 1st st is purled.
Cut yarn.

RIGHT ANGLE 2
Leg 1

Purl with dark gray; leg consists of 10 sts and 20 ridges.
With WS facing you and dark gray, K-CO 10 sts as extension of the 20 sts on needle (photo E).
Row 1 (WS): P9, p2tog; turn.
Row 2 (RS): Sl 1 pwise, purl to end of row; turn.
Row 3 (WS): Sl 1 kwise, p8, sl 1, k1,

psso; turn.
Rep Rows 2-3 until there are 20 ridges on both RS and WS. The last row is on RS.
The working yarn is at left side (photo F).

Leg 2

Continue from Leg 1. The leg consists of 30 sts and 10 ridges.
Row 1 (WS), pick up and purl: Sl 1 kwise, p9, continue pick up and purl 22 sts over Right Angle 2: 1 st before every ridge, 1 st after last ridge and 1 st in corner loop (= 32 sts, photo G).
Row 2 (RS): Sl 1 pwise, p19, p2tog, purl to end of row (= 30 sts); turn.
Row 3: Sl 1 kwise, purl to end of row; turn.

Row 4: *Sl 1 kwise, purl to end of row; turn.*
Rep Rows 3-4 until leg 2 has 10 ridges on both RS and WS; end with k1.

RIGHT ANGLE 3
Work as for Right Angle 1 with **knit**, using medium gray. Change to circular when comfortable.

Leg 1
Work as for Right Angle 1, Leg 1, but work 10 sts and 30 ridges.

Leg 2
Work as for Right Angle 1, Leg 2, with 42 sts on pick-up row, decreasing to 40 sts on next row. Work 10 ridges.

RIGHT ANGLE 4
*Work as for Right Angle 2 with **purl**, using light gray.*

Leg 1
Work as for Right Angle 2, Leg 1, but with 40 ridges.

Leg 2
Work as for Right Angle 2, Leg 2, beginning with 52 sts, decreasing to 50 sts on first row. Work until there are 10 ridges on RS and 9 ridges on WS. BO.

Now you've completed a large square.

RIGHT ANGLE PILLOW COVER

Make 4 large squares. Join them into one large square for a lovely pillow cover. Two of the squares are made as for the swatch in School 4, but, the colors have been changed a bit for the other two. Finally, you'll knit an edging around the cover and sew on the backing.

FINISHED MEASUREMENTS
Without edging, 15¾ x 15¾ in / 40 x 40 cm

MATERIALS
Yarn: CYCA #3 (DK, light worsted) Filcolana Pernilla (100% pure new wool, 191 yd/175 m / 50 g)

Yarn Colors and Amounts:
Acacia Heather 825 (curry)
Charcoal Heather 956 (charcoal)
Medium Gray Heather 955 (dark gray)
Light Gray Heather 954 (medium gray)
Very Light Gray Heather 957 (light gray)

Needles: U. S. size 2.5 / 3 mm: dpn and 48 in / 120 cm circular
Crochet Hook: U. S. size D-3 / 3 mm

Notions: Insert pillow, 15¾ x 15¾ in / 40 x 40 cm, fleece fabric for backing (www. stofogstil.dk), 16½ x 16½ in / 42 x 42 cm

GAUGE
24 sts and 52 rows/26 ridges in garter st = 4 x 4 in / 10 x 10 cm.
1 large square = 8 x 8 in / 20 x 20 cm
Adjust needle size to obtain correct gauge if necessary.

INSTRUCTIONS

Technique
The pattern is based on School 4 (page 70), and the diagram on page 76. Learn the technique by making the entire School 4 swatch or part of it.

Diagram
1 square = 1 stitch and 1 ridge/2 knit rows.

LARGE SQUARES 1 AND 2
Work entire School 4 swatch but do not bind off when finishing. Place sts on a holder.

LARGE SQUARE 3
Work as for School 4 swatch, using light gray, medium gray, dark gray, curry, and charcoal. Place sts on a holder.

LARGE SQUARE 4
Work as for School 4 swatch, using light gray, charcoal, curry, medium gray, and dark gray.

DIAGRAM FOR RIGHT ANGLE PILLOW COVER

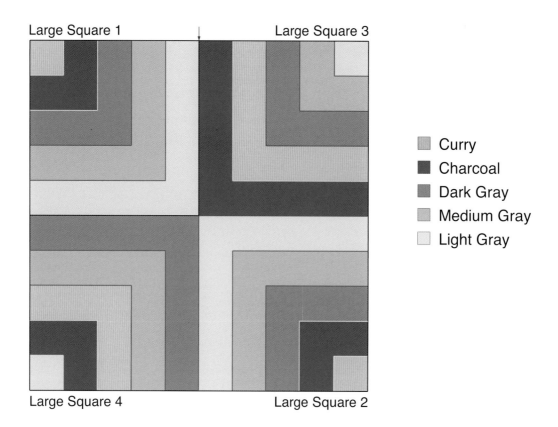

Large Square 1   Large Square 3

Large Square 4   Large Square 2

■ Curry
■ Charcoal
■ Dark Gray
■ Medium Gray
■ Light Gray

FINISHING

Crochet the 4 large squares together with charcoal and crochet hook U. S. D-3 / 3 mm (see Joining on page 185). Arrange squares as on diagram.

Large Squares 1 and 4: Place sts of Large Square 1 on a dpn. Fold Large Square 1 down over Large Square 4 with right sides facing, so sts lie at front and parallel to edge sts of Large Square 4. Crochet each st of Large Square 1 together with corresponding edge st of Large Square 4. Unfold panel.

Large Squares 2 and 3: Place sts of Large Square 2 on a dpn. Fold Large Square 2 down over Large Square 3 with right sides facing, and turn them so sts on needle lie at front and parallel to edge sts of Large Square 3. Crochet live sts together with edge sts one by one.
Place sts of Large Square 3 on a dpn.
Fold Large Squares 1 and 4 over Large Squares 3 and 2 with right sides facing. Begin joining at top between Large Squares 1 and 3 (at red arrow), where edge sts of Large Square 1 lie in front of sts of Large Square 3. Crochet edge sts together with live sts one by one along Large Squares 4 and 2, where sts of Large Square 4 lie in front of edge sts of Large Square 2.

EDGING

Work as for Garter Stitch Edging with 1 Edge Stitch, page 180, as follows:

Ridges
Rnd 1, pick up and knit:
Begin between 2 squares and, with curry and long circular, pick up and knit sts all around (approx. 100 sts per side).
Rnd 2: Purl.

Garter Stitch Edging with 1 Edge Stitch
Change to charcoal. K-CO 6 sts on left needle (where pick up and knit row began), and work edging but do not BO when finishing. Join live sts with cast-on row sts.

BACKING
Turn seam allowance to wrong side and stitch to pillow cover inside edge sts, leaving enough space to insert pillow. Insert pillow and then close backing.

Ridges
Rnd 1, pick up and knit:
Begin between 2 squares and, with curry and long circular, pick up and knit sts all around (approx. 100 sts per side).
Rnd 2: Purl.

Garter Stitch Edging with 1 Edge Stitch
Change to charcoal. K-CO 6 sts on left needle (where pick up and knit row began), and work edging but do not BO when finishing. Join live sts with cast-on row sts.

BACKING
Turn seam allowance to wrong side and stitch to pillow cover inside edge sts, leaving enough space to insert pillow. Insert pillow and then close backing.

RIGHT ANGLE JACKET

An apparently simple jacket… However, one leg of the right angle has 10 stitches and the other leg has 10 ridges. It is worked alternately in knit and purl, in one direction and then in the opposite direction. This alternating method of knitting gives the jacket structure and makes it sturdier. Best of all, it's beautiful and fun to knit.

SIZE
Medium/Large

FINISHED MEASUREMENTS
Chest: 52¾ in / 134 cm
Length: 23¾ in / 60 cm

MATERIALS
Yarn: CYCA #3 (DK, light worsted) Filcolana Pernilla (100% pure new wool, 191 yd/175 m / 50 g)
Yarn Colors and Amounts:
Fisherman Blue Heather 818 (dark blue): 150 g
Storm Blue Heather 814 (petroleum): 100 g
Aqua Mist Heather 808 (turquoise): 150 g
Granite Heather 812 (gray-blue): 100 g
Raindrop Heather 819 (mint): 100 g
Acacia Heather 825 (curry): 100 g

Needles: U. S. size 2.5 / 3 mm: 2 dpn and 2 x 24 in / 60 cm circulars
U. S. size 1.5 / 2.5 mm: 1 dpn and 24 and 48 in / 60 and 120 cm circulars

Notions: locking ring markers, 6 buttons

GAUGE
24 sts and 52 rows/26 ridges in garter st on larger needles = 4 x 4 in / 10 x 10 cm.
1 strip/right angle with 10 sts = approx. 1½ in / 4 cm
Adjust needle size to obtain correct gauge if necessary.

INSTRUCTIONS

Technique
The pattern is based on School 4 (page 70), and the diagrams on pages 80 and 83. Learn the technique by making the entire School 4 swatch.
Both front pieces and back begin with a rectangle instead of a square.

Diagram
The arrows indicate stitch direction. The gray lines at each corner show the transition from Leg 1 to Leg 2.

Ridges
When the pattern states that there should be 10 ridges, it means that there should be 10 ridges on both RS and WS.

Rule of Thumb
Always begin a new right angle where the previous one ended. The yarn should always hang at the side or in front—never at the center of the work.

Left Back **Right Back**

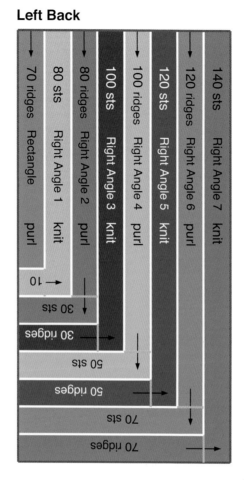
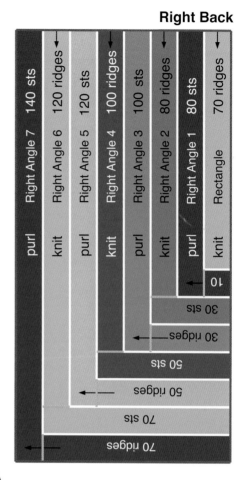

Center back

Legend:
- ■ Dark Blue
- ■ Petroleum
- ■ Turquoise
- ■ Gray-Blue
- ■ Mint
- ■ Curry

Left Back labels (top row): 70 ridges / 80 sts / 80 ridges / 100 sts / 100 ridges / 120 sts / 120 ridges / 140 sts

Left Back middle row: Rectangle / Right Angle 1 / Right Angle 2 / Right Angle 3 / Right Angle 4 / Right Angle 5 / Right Angle 6 / Right Angle 7

Left Back bottom row: purl / knit / purl / knit / purl / knit / purl / knit

Left Back inner labels: 10 → / 30 sts / 30 ridges / 50 sts / 50 ridges / 70 sts / 70 ridges

Right Back labels (top row): 140 sts / 120 ridges / 120 sts / 100 ridges / 100 sts / 80 ridges / 80 sts / 70 ridges

Right Back middle row: Right Angle 7 / Right Angle 6 / Right Angle 5 / Right Angle 4 / Right Angle 3 / Right Angle 2 / Right Angle 1 / Rectangle

Right Back bottom row: purl / knit / purl / knit / purl / knit / purl / knit

Right Back inner labels: 10 / 30 sts / 30 ridges / 50 sts / 50 ridges / 70 sts / 70 ridges

Left back turned upside down

LEFT BACK

Turn the diagram upside down, as in the photo of the finished back. The first figure, a rectangle, is worked as for the corner square in School 4, but continues until it becomes a rectangle.

The rectangle, as well as all right angles beginning at the shoulder (Right Angles 2, 4, and 6) are **purled** following the diagram. All right angles on jacket's side (Right Angles 1, 3, 5, and 7) are **knitted** following the diagram. On Leg 2 for all right angles, **always** pick up 2 extra sts on pick-up and knit/purl rows—they will be eliminated on Row 2.

RECTANGLE

*With gray-blue and dpn U. S. 2.5 / 3 mm, K-CO (with 2 beg sts) 10 sts and **purl** back and forth as for School 4's corner square, page 70.*

Row 1 (RS): *Purl across.*
Row 2 (WS): *Sl 1 kwise, purl to end of row.*
Row 3 (RS): *Sl 1 kwise, purl to end of row.*
Rep Rows 2-3 until there are 70 ridges on both RS and WS. The last row is on WS, so the yarn hangs at right side of work.

RIGHT ANGLE 1

Knit with curry as for School 4, Right Angle 1.

Leg 1

K-CO 10 sts as an extension of the rectangle's 10 sts on the needle.
Row 1 (RS): K9, p2tog (= 10 sts); turn.
Row 2 (WS): Sl 1 kwise, knit to end of row; turn.
Row 3 (RS): Sl 1 pwise, k8, p2tog; turn.
Rep Rows 2-3 until there are 10 ridges on both RS and WS. The last row is on WS, and the yarn hangs at right side of work.

Leg 2

Change to shorter circular U. S. 2.5 / 3 mm.
Row 1 (RS), pick up and knit: Sl 1 pwise and k9 over leg 1, pick up and knit 72 sts along rectangle: 1 st **before** each ridge, 1 after last ridge, and 1 in corner loop (= 82 sts).
Row 2 (WS): Sl 1 pwise, k2tog, knit until 11 sts rem, k2tog, knit to end of row (= 80 sts).
Row 3: Sl 1 pwise, knit to end of row.

Row 4: Sl 1 pwise, knit to end of row.
Rep Rows 3-4 until there are 10 ridges on both RS and WS. The last row is on RS.

RIGHT ANGLE 2

Purl with turquoise as for School 4, Right Angle 2.

Leg 1

Holding work in left hand with WS facing you, with turquoise, K-CO 10 sts as an extension of Right Angle 1's sts.
Row 1 (WS): *P9, sl 1, k1, psso; turn.*
Row 2 (RS): *Sl 1 pwise, purl to end of row.*
Row 3 (WS): *Sl 1 kwise, p8, sl 1, k1, psso; turn.*
Rep Rows 2-3 until there are 80 ridges on both RS and WS. The last row is on RS.

Leg 2

Row 1 (WS), pick up and purl: *Sl 1 kwise and p9, pick up and purl 22 sts along Right Angle 1: 1 st before each ridge, 1 after last ridge, and 1 in corner loop (= 32 sts).*
Row 2 (RS): *Sl 1 kwise, p2tog, purl until 11 sts rem, p2tog, purl to end of row (= 30 sts).*
Row 3: *Sl 1 kwise, purl to end of row.*
Row 4: *Sl 1 kwise, purl to end of row.*
Rep Rows 3-4 until there are 10 ridges on both RS and WS. The last row is on WS.

RIGHT ANGLE 3

Knit with dark blue as for School 4, Right Angle 3.

Leg 1

Work with 10 sts and 30 ridges.

Leg 2

Work with 10 ridges and 102 sts, decreasing to 100 sts on first row.

RIGHT ANGLE 4

Purl with mint as for School 4, Right Angle 4.

Leg 1

Work with 10 sts and 100 ridges.

Leg 2

Work with 10 ridges and 52 sts, decreasing to 50 sts on first row.

Continue with Right Angles 5, 6, and 7 with, respectively, petroleum, gray-blue, and turquoise as shown on diagram on page 80. End Right Angle 7 when there are 10 ridges on RS and 9 ridges on WS. Cut yarn and leave sts on needle.

RIGHT BACK

Turn diagram upside down so shoulder points downward.

RECTANGLE

Corresponds to rectangle on left back, but is **knitted** with mint. The first and last rows are on RS; turn.

RIGHT ANGLE 1

Purl with dark blue on dpn U. S. 2.5 / 3 mm.

Whole back, after the two pieces have been joined.

Leg 1

Holding work in left hand with WS facing you, K-CO 10 sts as an extension of rectangle's 10 sts.

Row 1 (WS): *P9, sl 1, k1, psso.*

Row 2 (RS): *Sl 1 pwise, purl to end of row.*

Row 3 (WS): *11 kwise, p8, sl 1, k1, psso.*

Rep Rows 2-3 until there are 10 ridges and only 10 sts rem of dark blue. End with a RS row. Change to U. S. 2.5 / 3 mm, 24 in / 60 cm circular.

Leg 2

Row 1 (WS), pick up and purl: *Sl 1 kwise and p9 across leg 1, pick up and purl 72 sts along rectangle: 1 st before each ridge, 1 after last ridge, and 1 in corner loop (= 82 sts).*

Row 2 (RS): *Sl 1 kwise, p2tog, purl*

until 11 sts rem, p2tog, purl to end of row (= 80 sts).

Row 3: *Sl 1 kwise, purl to end of row.*

Row 4: *Sl 1 kwise, purl to end of row.*

Rep Rows 3-4 until there are 10 ridges on RS. The last row is on WS.

RIGHT ANGLE 2

Knit with turquoise.

Leg 1

K-CO 10 sts as an extension of Right Angle 1's sts.

Row 1 (RS): K9, p2tog; turn.

Row 2 (WS): Sl 1 kwise, knit to end of row.

Row 3 (RS): Sl pwise, k8, p2tog; turn.

Rep Rows 2-3 until there are 80 ridges and 10 mint sts rem. The last row is on WS.

Leg 2

Row 1 (RS), pick up and knit: Sl 1 pwise and k9 over Leg 1, pick up and knit 22 sts along Right Angle 2; turn.

Row 2 (WS): Sl 1 pwise, k2tog, knit until 11 sts rem, k2tog, knit to end of row.

Row 3: Sl 1 pwise, knit to end of row.

Row 4: Sl 1 pwise, knit to end of row.

Rep Rows 3-4 until there are 10 ridges. The last row is on RS.

RIGHT ANGLE 3

Purl corresponding to Right Angle 1, but with gray-blue and 1 dpn U. S. 2.5 / 3 mm to help with Leg 1.

Leg 1

Holding work in left hand with WS facing you, K-CO 10 sts. Work 30 ridges.

Leg 2

Work with 10 ridges and 102 sts, decreasing to 100 sts on first row.

RIGHT ANGLE 4

Knit corresponding to Right Angle 2, but with petroleum.

Leg 1

10 sts and 100 ridges.

Leg 2

Work with 52 sts, decreasing to 50 sts on first row.
Continue with Right Angles 5, 6, and 7 in colors shown on diagram.
End Right Angle 7 when there are

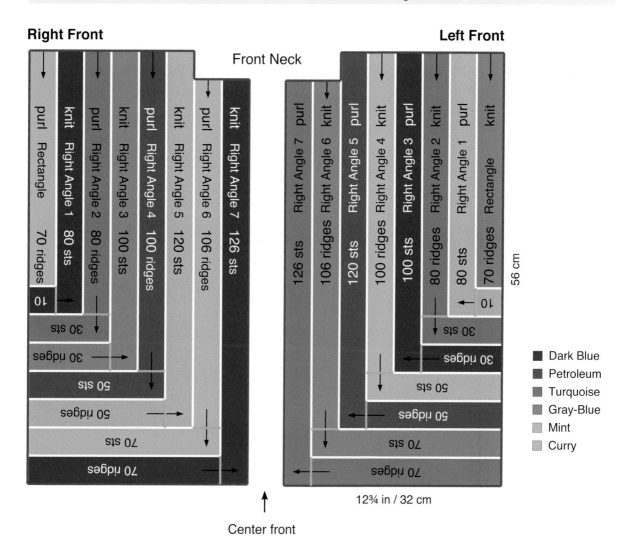

Right Front

Left Front

Front Neck

Center front

12¾ in / 32 cm

56 cm

Legend:
- Dark Blue
- Petroleum
- Turquoise
- Gray-Blue
- Mint
- Curry

10 ridges on RS and 9 on WS.

JOINING THE 2 SIDES OF BACK
Hold right and left sides of back with right sides facing and needles parallel. Using dpn U. S. 2.5 / 3 mm, join pieces with three-needle bind-off (see page 184).

LEFT FRONT
Work as for right back but in colors shown on diagram. Right Angles 6

and 7 are shorter on front to shape neckline.

RIGHT ANGLE 6
Place top 14 sts of Right Angle 5 onto a holder. Use the 15th st as a beg st and K-CO 10 sts with gray-blue. Work Leg 1 along Right Angle 5. Work Leg 2 as for Leg 2 of right back, Right Angle 6.

RIGHT ANGLE 7
Leg 2 is shorter than Right Angle 5's Leg 2.
End by leaving sts on needle or slip onto a holder for edging.

RIGHT FRONT
Work as for left back but in colors shown on diagram.

RIGHT ANGLE 6
Place top 14 sts of Right Angle 5

onto a holder for front neck. Use the 15th st as a beg st and K-CO 10 sts with mint. Work Leg 1 along Right Angle 5. Work Leg 2 as for Right Angle 6 on back.

RIGHT ANGLE 7

Leg 2 is shorter than Right Angle 5's Leg 2.

End by leaving sts on needle or slip onto a holder for edging.

RIGHT SHOULDER

Work shoulder along right front's top side (from Right Angle 5 to and including rectangle) as follows:

Row 1 (RS), pick up and knit: With dark blue and U. S. 2.5 / 3 mm, 24 in / 60 cm circular, pick up and knit 10 sts along each right angle and 10 sts along rectangle (= 60 sts). Work back and forth.

Row 2 (WS): Sl 1 pwise, k2tog, knit to end of row (= 60 sts).

Row 3: Sl 1 pwise, knit to end of row.

Row 4: Sl 1 pwise, knit to end of row.

Rep Rows 3-4 until there are 10 ridges on RS and 9 on WS. The last row is on WS.

Do not bind off; instead, use Kitchener st to join right shoulder with right back.

Alternatively, bind off and join pieces with mattress st.

LEFT SHOULDER

Work as for right shoulder along top side of left front (from rectangle to and including Right Angle 5). Join pieces with same method as for right shoulder.

SLEEVES

The sleeves are worked from the top down in stripes. See Sleeves on page 187.

Stripes

9 ridges/18 rows with each of the following colors: petroleum, mint, turquoise, dark blue, gray-blue, petroleum, mint, turquoise, dark blue, gray-blue, petroleum, and dark blue for edging.
Always begin a new color on RS.

With petroleum and U. S. 2.5 / 3 mm, 24 in / 60 cm circular, K-CO 104 sts (with 2 beg sts) and work back and forth.
Row 1 (WS): Knit across.
Row 2 (WS): Sl 1 pwise, knit to end of row.
Row 3 (WS): Sl 1 pwise, knit to end of row.
Rep Rows 2-3 throughout, and *at the same time*, on every 8th row, decrease as follows:
Alternate decreasing:
at center of row: K2tog, k2, sl 1, k1, psso, and **at beginning and end of row:** Sl 1 pwise, k1, k2tog,

knit until 4 sts rem, sl 1, k1, psso, k2. Decrease as est until 56 sts rem. Continue in stripes until sleeve is 15¾ in / 40 cm long (99 ridges) or desired length. The last row is on WS and is worked with U. S. 1.5 / 2.5 mm, 24 in / 60 cm circular.

Edging

Change to dark blue and work back and forth using U. S. 1.5 / 2.5 mm dpn to help; begin with K-CO 7 sts as an extension of the 56 sts on circular.
Work Garter Stitch Edging with 2 Edge Stitches, page 181.
BO when only 7 sts rem.

Make second sleeve the same way.

FINISHING

Seaming left side: From each side and in towards center, count 47 cast-on sts on top of sleeve. Pm so there are 10 cast-on loops between markers, corresponding to shoulder. Count, respectively, 47 ridges down from shoulder on back and front and pm. Seam sleeve in from marker and up, join shoulder

Bind a ring: Cut a short piece of yarn, fold it, and tie it into a ring. Place ring on needle like a stitch.

Place marker (pm): Cut a short piece of yarn, place it around a stitch, and knot it loosely.

with the 10 cast-on loops between markers and continue along the last 47 sts from marker and down. Seam sleeve from the top down, leaving last 4 in / 10 cm open. Seam side.
Seaming at right side: Pm and seam as for left side.

EDGING AND BUTTON CLOSURES

Work edging as for Ribbed Edging, page 183, with buttonholes. First, work left side and then right.

There are no edge sts; the two sides' edges are sewn together, centered on the outermost sts.

Notches and points: There are two corners turned in at the front neck; I call them notches. There are also two corners at top and bottom of the front bands which point downwards—they are points.

LEFT SIDE
Ridges
Row 1 (RS), pick up and knit:
With dark blue and U. S. 1.5 / 2.5 mm, 48 in / 120 cm circular, beginning at back neck, pick up and knit sts on RS:
Center back: 1 st between dark blue and turquoise,
Back neck: 20 sts over Right Angles 7 and 6,
Back notch: bind a ring and place it on corner row between 2 sts,

Shoulder: 11 sts (1 st for each ridge and 1 after),
Front neck: place the 14 held sts onto dpn and knit, front notch: bind a ring and place it on needle in corner between 2 sts,
Neck base: 20 sts;
Top point: 1 e-inc and place marker around increase,
Front edge: 126 sts,
Lower point: 1 e-inc and place marker around increase,
Front bottom: 80 sts towards side seam,
Back, bottom: 80 sts to center back.

Row 2 (WS): Knit, but, in each of the 2 notches, k2tog (1 st before and 1 st after notch). Untie rings and, instead, bind them around each of the 2 joined sts. Cut yarn.
Row 3 (WS): Begin a lower edge of center back on WS, and, with turquoise:
Back and front, bottom: purl to lowest point, and *at the same time* decrease 6 sts evenly spaced across (= 154 sts),
Lowest point: 1 e-inc, p1 (st in marker), 1 e-inc,
Front edge: purl, and *at the same time* decrease 5 sts evenly spaced across (= 121 sts),
Top point: 1 e-inc, p1 (st in marker), 1 e-inc,
Front neck, base: p17,
First notch: p2tog, p1 (st in marker), p2tog,
Front neck, side and shoulder: p19,
Back notch: p2tog, p1 (st in marker), p2tog,
Back neck: p17,
Center back: p1.

Ribbing
Row 4 (RS): Beginning with k1, work in p1, k1 ribbing. Make sure to knit the st in each point and notch.
Row 5 (WS): Knit over knit and purl over purl and work 1 e-inc on both sides of st with maker in the 2 points (marker) and p2tog on each side of sts with marker in the 2 notches.
Gradually, the sts in the points are eliminated and the sts can be worked in ribbing.

Rows 6 and 8: Work as for Row 4.
Rows 7 and 9: Work as for Row 5. BO in ribbing, making sure bind-off is not too tight.

RIGHT SIDE
Ridges
Rows 1 and 2: With turquoise, work as for left side but in the opposite sequence: begin at lower center of back (at bottom).
Row 3: Change to dark blue and continue as for left side, but in opposite sequence.

Ribbing
Row 4: When 4th row is worked, pm where buttonholes will be. Count 3 sts down from top marker and pm, place 5 more markers with 18 sts between each.

Buttonholes
Row 5 (RS): Sl 1 pwise, k1, k2tog, yo twice, p2tog; turn.
Row 6 (WS): Sl 1 kwise, k1 and k1tbl in double yo, knit to end of row.

Continue edging to next marker and make a buttonhole.
Rep until all 6 buttonholes have been worked.

Rows 7-9: Work as for left side, BO.

Sew on buttons opposite buttonholes.

5
STAIRCASES

STAIRCASES

SCHOOL 5

Knitting up and down staircases is downright funny—and useful for shawls, sweaters, and much more. Staircases can be knitted as here, on the diagonal, or horizontally, as in School 6 (page 110). Staircases can be worked alternately in purl and knit, step by step, staircase by staircase. Each staircase consists of steps, formed as rectangles, but ends or begins with a "half" step, to form a square.

FINISHED MEASUREMENTS
Whole Swatch: 7½ x 7½ in / 19 x 19 cm
Single Section: 1 step wide and 2 steps high, approx. 2 x 2 in / 5 x 5 cm

MATERIALS
Yarn: CYCA #3 (DK, light worsted) Filcolana Pernilla (100% pure new wool, 191 yd/175 m / 50 g)
Yarn Colors and Amounts:
Charcoal Heather 956 (charcoal)
Willow Heather 822 (khaki)
Lavender Gray Heather 815 (light purple)
Acacia Heather 825 (curry)

Needles: U. S. size 2.5 / 3 mm: 2 dpn and 24 in / 60 cm circular

SWATCH

Stitches and Ridges
A step can have any even number of stitches. The number of ridges should be half the stitch count of the step.
Each step in this swatch has 12 sts and 6 ridges.

Rule of Thumb
Always begin a staircase where the last-knitted one ended. The yarn should always hang at outer edge of the last-knitted stitch, ready to be the beginning stitch for the next staircase.

STAIRCASE 1
The first staircase consists of only 2 steps: a "whole" and a "half."
*It is **purled** in a single color, charcoal.*
Direction of work: bottom up towards right.

Step 1
Purl beginning step—a rectangle.
With charcoal and dpn, K-CO 12 sts (with 2 beg sts).
Row 1 (RS): Purl across.
Row 2 (WS): Sl 1 kwise, purl to end of row.
Row 3 (WS): Sl 1 kwise, purl to end of row.
Rep Rows 2-3 until there are 6 ridges on both RS and WS, after a WS row (photo A).
When RS faces you, the yarn end is on the left side and the working yarn at right.

Step 2
Purl end step—a square.
Continue over the first 6 sts. The other 6 sts rem on needle.
Row 1 (RS): Sl 1 kwise, p5; turn.
Row 2 (WS): Sl 1 kwise, p5; turn.
Rep Rows 1-2 until there are 6 ridges on both RS and WS, after a

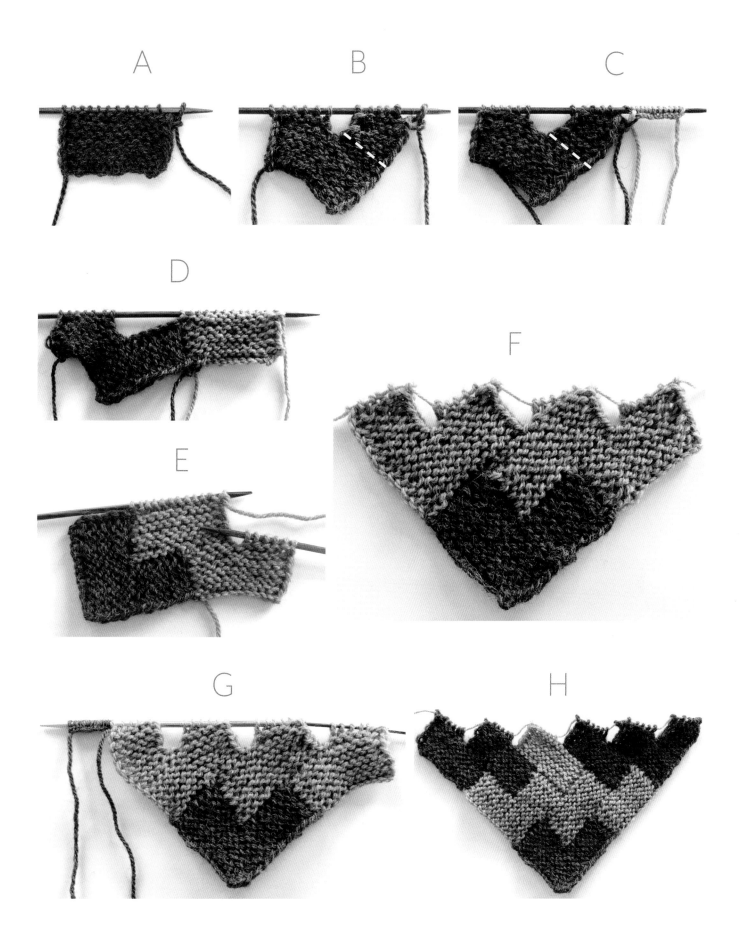

A   B   C

D

F

E

G   H

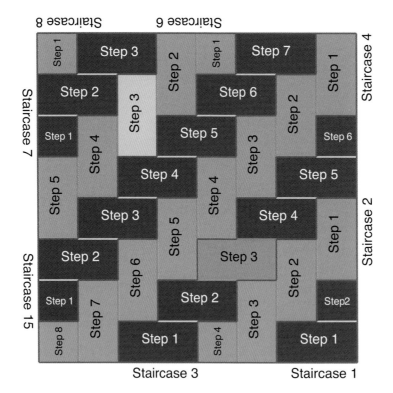

Legend:
- ■ Charcoal
- ■ Khaki
- ■ Light Purple
- ■ Curry

WS row (photo B). There are a total of 12 ridges on RS and WS of Steps 1 and 2. The yarn hangs at right side. Cut yarn.

STAIRCASE 2

Knit this staircase with charcoal. Direction of work: from right and down to left.

Turn chart one quarter to the right (clockwise).

Step 1

Knit beginning step—a rectangle. Holding work with RS facing you, begin where last staircase ended (i.e., where yarn hangs). Use last st of previous staircase as new beginning st. K-CO 12 sts as an extension of previous staircase (photo C).

Do not count beginning st as part of the 12 sts.

Row 1 (RS): K11, p2tog with last khaki st and first charcoal st; turn.

Row 2 (WS): Sl 1 kwise, knit to end of row; turn.

Row 3 (RS): Sl 1 pwise, k10, p2tog (with 1 khaki st and1 charcoal st); turn.

Rep Rows 2-3 until there are 6 ridges on both RS and WS after a WS row.

There should now be 12 khaki and 6 charcoal sts (photo D).

Step 2

Knit intermediate step—a rectangle.

Row 1 (RS), pick up and knit: Sl 1 pwise, k11, pick up and knit 7 sts along step to left (here Staircase 1, Step 2): 1 st for every ridge (= 19 sts), holding yarn on left index finger, move last st to left needle and p2tog; turn.

Row 2 (WS): Sl 1 kwise, k5, p2tog, k5 (= 12 sts); turn.

Leave last 6 khaki sts to rest on right needle.

Row 3: Sl 1 pwise, k10, p2tog; turn.

Row 4: Sl 1 kwise, k11; turn.

Rep Rows 3-4, until this step consists of 6 ridges on RS and 5 on WS after a WS row (photo E).

Step 3

Knit intermediate step—a rectangle.

Row 1 (RS), pick up and knit: Sl 1 pwise, k11, pick up and knit 8 sts along step to left (here Staircase 1, Step 1): 1 st for every ridge and last st in corner loop (= 20 sts); turn.

Row 2 (WS): Sl 1 pwise, k2tog, k4, k2tog, k5 (= 12 sts); turn.

Row 3: Sl 1 pwise, k11; turn.
Row 4: Sl 1 kwise, k11; turn.
Rep Row 3-4, until this step consists of 6 ridges on RS and 5 on WS after a WS row.

Step 4

Knit end step—a square.
Row 1 (RS): Sl 1 pwise, knit across; turn.
Row 2 (WS): Sl 1 pwise, k5 and leave last 6 sts; turn.
Row 3: Sl 1 pwise, k5; turn.
Row 4: Sl 1 kwise, k5; turn.
Rep Row 3-4, until this step consists of 6 ridges on both RS and WS after a RS row. The yarn now hangs on left side (at edge).
Leave sts on needle and cut yarn (photo F).

Place piece on circular and work back and forth.

STAIRCASE 3

This staircase is **purled** with charcoal and one light purple step.
Direction of work: from left up to right.
Turn chart so text of Staircase 3 is upright.

Step 1

Purl beginning step—a rectangle.
With WS facing you, begin where last staircase ended. Use the last knitted st as a beginning st and K-CO 12 sts with charcoal as an extension of previous staircase (photo G, here on RS).
Row 1 WS): P11, sl 1, k1, psso (see page 172); turn.
Row 2 (RS): Sl 1 pwise, purl to end of row; turn.

Row 3 (WS): Sl 1 kwise, p10, sl 1, k1, psso; turn.
Rep Rows 2-3, until there are 6 ridges on both RS and WS after a RS row. The yarn now hangs on right side.

Step 2

Purl intermediate step—a rectangle.
Row 1 (WS), pick up and purl: Sl 1 kwise, p11, pick up and purl 7 sts along step to left (here Staircase 2, Step 4): 1 st for every ridge (= 19 sts), k2tog (hold yarn on left index finger, with yarn over needle, move last-worked st to left needle under yarn, take yarn back between the 2 needles and sl 1, k1, psso; turn.
Row 2 (RS): Sl 1 pwise, p5, p2tog, p5 (= 12 sts); turn.
Leave last unworked 6 charcoal sts to rest on right needle.
Row 3: Sl 1 kwise, p10, sl 1, k1, psso; turn.
Row 4: Sl 1 pwise, purl to end of row (= p11); turn.
Rep Row 3-4, until there are 6 ridges on RS and 5 on WS after a RS row.

Step 3

Purl intermediate step—a rectangle.
Row 1 (WS): Sl 1 kwise, p5 with charcoal. Cut charcoal and change to light purple, work rest of step as for Step 2.

Step 4

Purl intermediate step—a rectangle.
Row 1 (WS): Sl 1 kwise, p5 with light purple. Cut light purple, change to charcoal, and work rest of step 4 as for Step 2.

Step 5

Purl intermediate step—a rectangle.
Row 1 (WS), pick up and purl:
Sl 1 kwise, p11, pick up and purl 8 sts along step to left (here Staircase 2, Step 1): 1 st for every ridge and last st in corner loop (= 20 sts); turn.
Row 2 (RS): Sl 1 kwise, p2tog, p4, p2tog, p5; turn.
Row 3: Sl 1 kwise, purl to end of row; turn.
Row 4: Sl 1 kwise, purl to end of row; turn.
Rep Rows 3-4 over these 12 sts, leaving last 6 sts to rest until there are 6 ridges on RS and 5 on WS after a RS row.

Step 6

Purl end step—a square.
Work as for Staircase 1, Step 2 (photo H).

STAIRCASE 4

Knit this staircase with khaki.
Direction of work: from top right corner and down to left corner.

Step 1 is as for Staircase 2, Step 1.
Steps 2, 3, 4, 5, and 6: as for Staircase 2, Step 2.
Step 7 is as for Staircase 2, Step 3.
Step 8 is as for Staircase 2, Step 4 until there are 5 ridges on both RS and WS. BO on WS, knitting 1st st but leaving 6th st (= end st).

STAIRCASE 5

This staircase is **purled** with charcoal.
Direction of work: from left side and up to right.

Step 1

***Purl beginning step**—a square.*

***Row 1 (WS), pick up and purl:** P1
in end st of last staircase, pick up and
purl 6 sts along Step 8: 1 st for every
ridge (= 7 sts), move last st to left
needle (see Staircase 3, Step 2, Row 1)
and sl 1, k1, psso; turn.*

***Row 2 (RS):** Sl 1 pwise, p3, p2tog, p1
(= 6 sts); turn.*

***Row 3:** Sl 1 kwise, p4, sl 1, k1, psso;
turn.*

***Row 4:** Sl 1 pwise, purl to end of row;
turn.*

*Rep Rows 3-4, until there are 6 ridges
on RS and 5 on WS after a RS row.*

Step 2

***Purl intermediate step**—a
rectangle.*

***Row 1 (WS), pick up and purl:** Sl 1
kwise, p5, pick up and purl 7 sts along
step to left (here Staircase 4, Step 7):
1 st for every ridge, move last st to left
needle and p2tog; turn.*

***Row 2 (RS):** Sl 1 pwise, p5, p2tog,
p5 (= 12 sts); turn.*

***Row 3:** Sl 1 kwise, p10, sl 1, k1, psso;
turn.*

***Row 4:** Sl 1 pwise, purl to end of row;
(= p11) turn.*

*Rep Rows 3-4 until there are 6 ridges
on RS and 5 on WS after a RS row.*

*Continue with intermediate steps and
then an end step (a rectangle with 5
ridges on both RS and WS). BO 11 sts
pwise on RS, with first st as sl 1 kwise.
Leave last st on needle.*

STAIRCASE 6

Knit this staircase with khaki and a
single curry step.
Direction of work: from right and
down to left.

Step 1

Knit beginning step—a square.
Knit end st of previous staircase,
pick up and knit 6 sts in edge sts,
move last st to left needle, and
p2tog; turn.

Row 1 (WS): Sl 1 pwise, k3, k2og,
k1; turn.

Row 2 (RS): Sl 1 pwise, k4, p2tog;
turn.

Row 3 (WS): Sl 1 kwise, knit to end
of row; turn.

Rep Rows 2-3 until there are 6
ridges on RS and 5 on WS after a
WS row.

Step 2

Knit intermediate step—a
rectangle.

Row 1 (RS): Sl 1 pwise, k5, pick up
and knit 7 sts along last staircase
(here, Staircase 5, Step 6): 1 st for
every ridge (= 13 sts), holding yarn
on left index finger, move last st to
left needle, and p2tog; turn.

Row 2 (WS): Sl 1 pwise, k5, k2tog,
k5; turn.

Row 3: Sl 1 pwise, k10, p2tog; turn.

Row 4: Sl 1 pwise, knit to end of
row; turn.

Rep Rows 3-4 until there are 6
ridges on RS and 5 on WS after a
WS row.

Step 3

Knit intermediate step—a
rectangle.
Work as for Staircase 2, Step 2,
but knit first 6 sts with khaki and
change to curry.

Step 4

Knit intermediate step—a
rectangle.
Work as for Staircase 2, Step 2,
but knit first 6 sts with curry and
change to khaki.

Step 5

Knit intermediate step—a
rectangle.
A rectangle with 5 ridges on both
RS and WS. BO 11 sts kwise on RS,
slipping first st kwise. Leave last st
on needle.

STAIRCASE 7

*This staircase is **purled** with charcoal.
Direction of work: from left and up to
right.*

*Work as for Staircase 5, Steps 1, 2,
and 7. End as for Staircase 5.*

STAIRCASE 8

This staircase has only one step.
Work as for Staircase 4, Step 8
with 5 ridges on both RS and WS.
BO kwise on WS.

MARIE GRUBBE— LONG SHAWL

This shawl is especially pretty and lovely to wear. It is worked in one piece with staircases on the diagonal, and it's completely worth the time involved.

FINISHED MEASUREMENTS

Width: including edging, 19 in / 48 cm

Length: including edging, as measured from tip, approx. 64¾ in / 165 cm

MATERIALS

Yarn: CYCA #1 (fingering) Camarose Yaku 4/16 (100% mulesing-free high quality Merino wool, 219 yd/200 m / 50 g)

Yarn Colors and Amounts:
Black 1999: 250 g
Gray 1060: 150 g
Leftover silk yarns: 10 g each red, red-violet, lime, and curry

If you want to make the shawl with Yaku only, you'll also need colors
Coral 1112: 50 g
Magenta 1704: 50 g
Apple Green 1313: 50 g
Mustard Yellow: 50 g

Needles: U. S. size 2.5 / 3 mm: 2 dpn and 24 in / 60 cm circular U. S. size 1.5 / 2.5 mm: 1 short dpn and 24 and 40 in / 60 and 100 cm circulars

GAUGE

1 step (12 sts) in width and 2 steps in height, joined with another step = approx. 1¾ x 1¾ in / 4.5 x 4.5 cm
Adjust needle size to obtain correct gauge if necessary.

INSTRUCTIONS

Technique

The pattern is based on School 5 (page 90) and the diagram on page 98. Learn the technique by making the entire School 5 swatch, or only the first 4 staircases with the yarn and colors you'll use for the shawl. Those 4 staircases are the same as the beginning of this shawl, so you can measure the gauge using that section.

Diagram

Each step is 12 sts and 6 ridges on RS.

LONG SHAWL
STAIRCASES 1, 2, 3, AND 4

Work as for School 5's 4 staircases, but, here Staircase 1 is black, Staircase 2 is gray, Staircase 3 is black with a red step, and Staircase 4 is gray. Begin with dpn and change to circular when comfortable.

DIAGRAM FOR MARIE GRUBBE LONG SHAWL

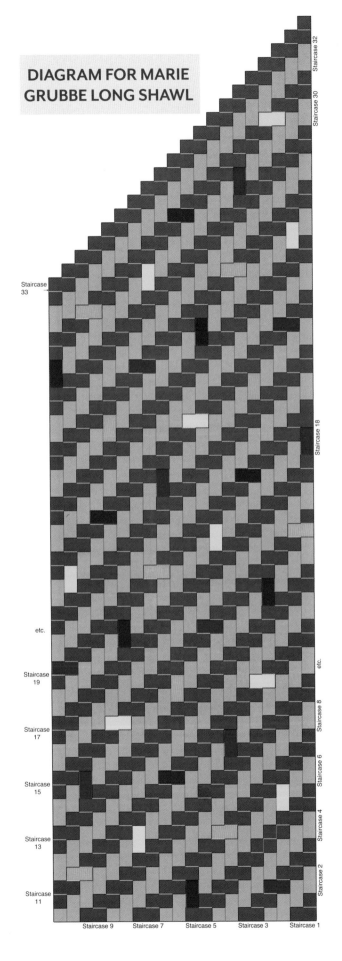

- ■ Black
- ■ Gray
- ■ Red
- ■ Red-Violet
- □ Lime
- ▨ Curry

About Marie Grubbe (1643-1718)

Marie Grubbe came from a noble family, and grew up on the Tjele estate. She first married Ulrik Frederik Gyldenløve, one of the kingdom's foremost men and the son of King Frederik 3, but the marriage did not prosper. She was married again, this time to a nobleman named Palle Dyre, but this was also not a happy marriage. She found love at last when she returned home to Tjele, where she encountered the estate's driver, Søren Sørensen Møller. They moved from place to place together and supported themselves with a little of everything—including, it was said, Marie dancing at the market for a few pennies per dance. Søren subsequently became the ferryman at Borrehuset at Grønsund, close to Stubbekøbing, which is where I live. He was not faithful to Marie, and in 1711, he shot a man and was condemned to forced labor on Bremerholm, where he died. In 1714-16, Marie was granted public assistance of 2 rigsdaler annually.

Ludvig Holberg, a famous Danish writer and thinker, met Marie when she fled south to escape the plague, and he observed that even then, she still loved her Søren.

This shawl's steps are reminiscent of the social ladder Marie climbed down, and the steps of love she rose up on.

These 4 staircases are on the lower right corner of diagram.

STAIRCASE 5
Purl with black as for School 5, Staircase 3, but longer.

STAIRCASE 6
Knit with gray, with lime for Step 3 and red-violet for Step 10.

STAIRCASES 7, 8, AND 9
Continue as est, following diagram.

STAIRCASE 10
Knit and end as for School 5, Staircase 4.

STAIRCASE 11
Purl and begin as for School 5, Staircase 5.

STAIRCASE 12
Knit as usual until there are 5 ridges on both RS and WS on last step. BO on WS (slipping first st kwise). Place last st on left needle.

Continue, following diagram through Staircase 33, or until shawl is desired length. Leave sts on needle.
NOTE: Staircase 18 begins with a red step.

FINISHING AFTER STAIRCASE 33
Turn piece so RS faces you and begin where Staircase 33 ended: bind off 5 sts, and then *pick up and knit 1 st in edge st after each ridge (6 total) on left side of step, *at the same time* as binding off. BO

sts of next step (6 total)*. Rep * to * until all the "sawtooth" edges have been bound off.
Weave in all ends.

EDGINGS

All edgings are knit with black as for Garter Stitch Edging with 2 Edge Stitches on page 181.
Edgings are not included on the diagram.

Edging Along the Short Side
Pick Up and Knit Row: With RS facing, using black and smaller circular, pick up and knit sts on short side. Pick up 1 st in corner, then 12 sts (1 in each edge st) along each staircase, first along Staircase 10 and then 9, 8, etc; ending with 1 st in corner (122 sts).
Knit 1 row.
K-CO 7 sts as an extension of row and work back and forth on circular and 1 smaller dpn.
Row 1 (RS): Sl 2 pwise, k4, p2tog; turn.
Row 2 (WS): Sl 1 kwise, k6; turn.
Rep Rows 1-2 throughout. After each RS row, 1 of the 122 sts is eliminated until, at last, only 7 sts rem. Work last row on WS. You are now at corner of Staircase 1 on longer side.

Edging Along the Longest Side
Pick Up and Knit Row: Place the 7 sts from short side onto smaller long circular. Knit the 7 sts of short side and continue by picking up and knitting 12 sts per step/staircase on long side (towards tip). Knit 1 row

back over all sts. K-CO 7 sts, and rep Rows 1-2 as on short side until 7 sts of edging rem.
Last Row (WS): Sl 1 kwise, k6.
Edging Top Step
Continue by knitting a bit longer over the 7 sts (photo A) with smaller dpn:
Row 1 (RS): Sl 2 pwise, k5.
Row 2 (WS): Sl 1 pwise, k6.
Rep Rows 1-2 until there are 5 ridges on RS; the last row is on WS. Finish as follows: Sl 2 pwise, draw first st over second, BO 5 sts. Pick up and knit sts along left side of top step, *at the same time* as binding off sts as for Staircase 33.

A

Edging Along Next-Longest Side (Left)
Pick Up and Knit Row: Begin next to Staircase 33 between Steps 1 and 2, at the little arrow on the diagram. Pick up and knit 6 sts along Step 1, and along whole side, 12 sts along each step/staircase; end with 6 sts along short edge, pick up and knit 1 extra st in corner. Sl 1 pwise, knit to end of row. K-CO 7 sts and work edging as for short side. BO on RS.

STAIRCASES JACKET

Here is a cropped but slightly wide jacket in neutral colors and with an exciting staircase motif that will make you feel elegant, well-dressed, and warm. It is entertaining to knit but you might need to bite your tongue at times.

SIZE
Medium

FINISHED MEASUREMENTS
Right/Left Back: before seaming, 11 x 16 in / 28 x 40.5 cm
Right/Left Front: before seaming, 11 x 16 in / 28 x 40.5 cm
Chest: 45¾ in / 116 cm
Total Length: 17¼ in / 44 cm
Sleeve Length: 17 in / 43 cm

MATERIALS
Yarn: CYCA #3 (DK, light worsted) Filcolana Pernilla (100% pure new wool, 191 yd/175 m / 50 g)
Yarn Colors and Amounts:
Charcoal Heather 956 (charcoal): 500 g
Willow Heather 822 (khaki): 300 g
Aqua Mint Heather 808 (turquoise): 10 g
Lavender Gray Heather 815 (light purple): 10 g
Parrot Green Heather 824 (green): 10 g
Acacia Heather 825 (curry): 10 g

Needles: U. S. size 2.5 / 3 mm: 2 dpn and 24 in / 60 cm circular
U. S. size 1.5 / 2.5 mm: 2 dpn and 24 and 40 in / 60 and 100 cm circulars

Notions: 6 buttons

GAUGE
1 step (12 sts) in width and 2 steps in height, joined with another step = approx. 1¾ x 1¾ in / 4.5 x 4.5 cm
On sleeves: 25 sts and 48 rows/24 garter ridges in garter st with larger needles = 4 x 4 in / 10 x 10 cm
Adjust needle size to obtain correct gauge if necessary.

INSTRUCTIONS
This jacket is worked in 6 pieces which are joined in finishing. Edgings are then knitted on. Begin with larger dpn and change to same size circular when comfortable.

Technique
The pattern is based on School 5 (page 94), and the diagrams on page 107. Learn the technique by making the entire School 5 swatch, or only the first 4 staircases with the yarn and colors you'll use for the jacket. Those 4 staircases are the same as the beginning of this jacket, so you can measure the gauge from that section.

Diagram
Turn diagrams as necessary. The starting point is where the red line is horizontal at top of the piece to be knitted. Each time you begin a new staircase, turn the diagram,

so the text "Staircase 2," "Staircase 3," etc., is upright.

Stitches and Ridges
Each step has 13 sts and 6 ridges on RS.

LEFT FRONT
is a large rectangle on the vertical. Begin so red line is horizontal at the top.

Direction of work
Always begin a staircase where previous staircase ended.
Purl staircases with charcoal go from bottom up and towards the right.
Knit staircases with khaki go from top down and towards the left.

STAIRCASES 1, 2, 3, AND 4
Work as for School 5's first 4 staircases, and in the same colors except for Staircase 3, Step 3, which will be turquoise. Each step should have 12 sts and 6 ridges on RS. These 4 staircases are at lower right corner of diagrams.

STAIRCASE 5
Purl with charcoal.
Work as for Staircase 3, but longer and in only color.

STAIRCASE 6
Knit with khaki, but work Step 4 with yellow and Step 9 with light purple. Work as for Staircase 2, but longer. Do not work last row of last step, but BO on RS when there are 5 ridges on both RS and WS. The yarn end hangs at side in lower left corner.

STAIRCASE 7
Purl with charcoal.
Work as for School 5, Staircase 5, but longer, and end as for Staircase 3.

STAIRCASE 8
Knit with khaki.
Begin as for School 5, Staircase 2, but end as for School's Staircase 6.

STAIRCASE 9
Purl with charcoal, but work step with green and step 9 with turquoise. *Begin as for School 5, Staircase 5, and end with a step not knitted together at right side. End by placing sts on a holder for later.*

STAIRCASE 10
Knit with khaki.
Begin as for School 5, Staircase 6, but longer.

STAIRCASE 11
Purl with charcoal.
Work as for School 5, Staircase 5, but longer. End by placing sts on a holder for later.

STAIRCASE 12
Knit with khaki, but work Step 4 with light purple.
Work as for School 5, Staircase 6.

STAIRCASE 13
Purl with charcoal.
Work as for School 5, Staircase 5, but shorter. End by placing sts on a holder for later.

STAIRCASE 14
Knit with khaki.
Work as for School 5, Staircase 6, Steps 1 and 2.
End as follows: Sl 1 kwise, BO 10 sts kwise on RS. Leave last st on needle.

RIGHT BACK
Turn chart so that the red line is at top.
Work to correspond to left front but with a different arrangement of contrast colors.

RIGHT FRONT
Is a large, horizontal rectangle. The diagram is turned and read horizontally.
Work following same principle as for left front. See colors on diagram.

LEFT BACK
Work as for right front. Turn diagram once more (so red line is at top). Use colors as shown on diagram.

SLEEVES
The sleeves are worked from the top down. See Sleeves on page 187.
With charcoal and larger circular, K-CO 108 sts (with 2 beg sts) and work back and forth.
Row 1 (WS): Knit.
Row 2 (WS): Sl pwise, knit to end

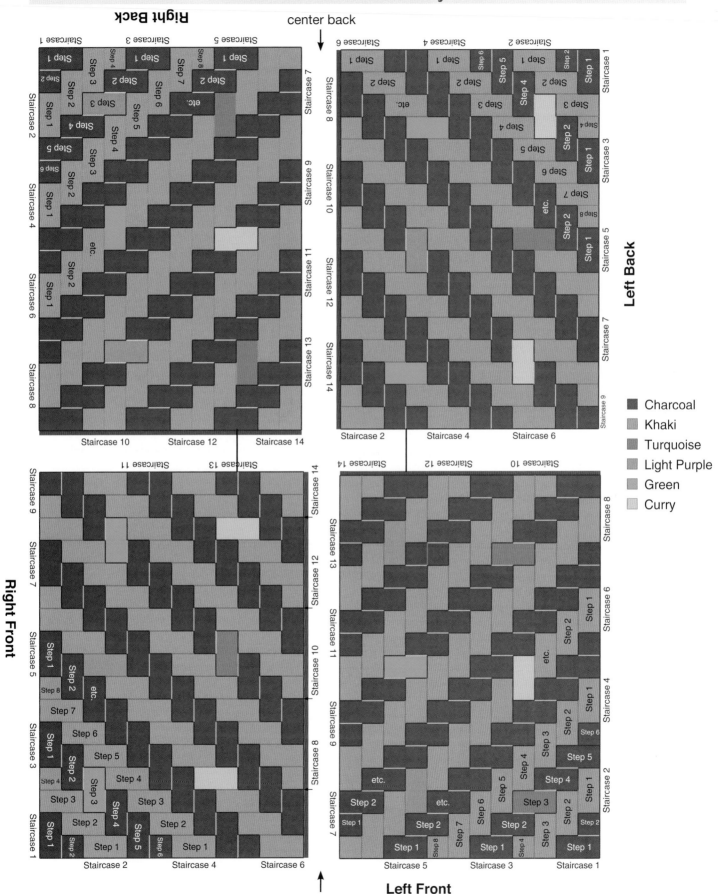

center back

Right Back

Staircase 1 · Staircase 3 · Staircase 5

Step 1 · Step 1 · Step 1 · Step 1
Step 2
Step 2 · Step 2 · Step 2
Step 3
Step 2 · Step 3 · Step 6 · Step 7
Step 3 · Step 4 · Step 5 · etc.
Step 1 · Step 4
Step 4 · Step 5
Step 5
Step 3
Step 2
Step 1
Step 2
Step 1
Step 2
Step 1
etc.

Staircase 2 · Staircase 4 · Staircase 6 · Staircase 8
Staircase 7 · Staircase 9 · Staircase 11 · Staircase 13

Staircase 10 · Staircase 12 · Staircase 14

Left Back

Staircase 6 · Staircase 4 · Staircase 2 · Staircase 1
Step 1 · Step 1 · Step 5 · Step 1 · Step 1
Step 2 · Step 2 · Step 4 · Step 2 · Step 2
etc. · Step 3 · Step 2 · Step 3
Step 4 · Step 2 · Step 4
Step 5 · Step 1
Step 6
Step 7
Step 2 · Step 8
Step 1

Staircase 8 · Staircase 10 · Staircase 12 · Staircase 14
Staircase 3 · Staircase 5 · Staircase 7 · Staircase 9

Staircase 2 · Staircase 4 · Staircase 6

Legend:
- ■ Charcoal
- ■ Khaki
- ■ Turquoise
- ■ Light Purple
- ■ Green
- ■ Curry

Right Front

Staircase 11 · Staircase 13 · Staircase 14

Staircase 9 · Staircase 7 · Staircase 12 · Staircase 10

Step 1 · Step 1 · etc.
Step 8 · Step 2
Step 7
Step 6 · Step 1
Step 5 · Step 2
Step 6 · Step 4 · Step 5
Step 1 · Step 2 · Step 3 · Step 4 · Step 3
Step 4 · Step 3 · Step 2
Step 3 · Step 3 · Step 2
Step 2 · Step 4 · Step 2
Step 1 · Step 1 · Step 5 · Step 6 · Step 1
Step 2

Staircase 1 · Staircase 3 · Staircase 5
Staircase 2 · Staircase 4 · Staircase 6

Left Front

Staircase 14 · Staircase 12 · Staircase 10
Staircase 13 · Staircase 11 · Staircase 9 · Staircase 7

Staircase 8 · Staircase 6 · Staircase 4 · Staircase 2
Step 1 · Step 2 · Step 1
etc. · Step 2
Step 1 · Step 3 · Step 6
Step 4 · Step 5
Step 5 · Step 4
etc. · Step 3 · Step 1
Step 2 · etc. · Step 2
Step 1 · Step 2 · Step 7 · Step 6 · Step 3 · Step 2
Step 1 · Step 8 · Step 1 · Step 4 · Step 1

Staircase 5 · Staircase 3 · Staircase 1

center front

Left Front

of row.

Row 3 (RS): Sl pwise, knit to end of row.

Rep Rows 2-3 throughout, and *at the same time*, on every 8th row, decrease as follows:

Alternate decreasing:
at center of row: K2tog k2, sl 1, k1, psso, and **at beginning and end of row:** Sl 1 pwise, k1, k2tog, knit until 4 sts rem, sl 1, k1, psso, k2. Decrease as est until 56 sts rem. Continue until sleeve is 17 in / 43 cm long (110 ridges) or desired length. The last row is on WS.

Double-knit Edging

K-CO 5 sts as an extension of 1st row:

Row 1 (RS): K1, sl 1 pwise, k1, sl 1 pwise, p2tog; turn.

Row 2 (WS): Sl 1 kwise, k1, sl 1 pwise, k1, sl 1 pwise; turn.

Rep 1-2 until only 5 sts rem.
BO on RS, and *at the same time*, k2tog 2 times.

Knit second sleeve the same way.

ASSEMBLING JACKET

Now join the 4 pieces, partly with a back band "center back" between the 2 sides of the back, partly with 2 shoulder pieces.

BACK BAND

With charcoal and larger circular, pick up and knit 95 sts along **right back**, where it faces the center. Begin at top: pick up and knit 1 st in corner, 11 sts for each staircase, 5 sts along lowest step, and 1 st in corner; turn work and K-CO 6 sts

(sts of band); turn again, and pick up and knit 95 sts along **left back:** 1 st in corner, 5 sts along lowest step, 11 sts for each staircase, and 1 st in corner. Cut yarn. Now work back and forth on circular.

Begin by slipping 95 sts of right back and then continue as follows:

Row 1 (RS): K5, p2tog (6 sts of band and first st of left back); turn.

Row 2 (WS): Sl 1 kwise, 5, sl 1, k1, psso (with last st of band and 1ˢᵗ st of left back); turn.

Row 3: Sl 1 pwise, k5, p2tog; turn.

Row 4: Sl 1 kwise, k5, sl 1, k1, psso; turn.

Rep Rows 3-4 until all vertical sts have been eliminated and only 6 sts rem. Place sts on a locking ring marker.

Now 2 pieces have been joined.

LEFT SHOULDER

Begin on left front where the Staircase 9 ends and, with charcoal and larger circular, pick up and knit 51 sts: 1 st in corner, 11 sts for each of first 4 staircases, 6 sts along first half of next staircase (marked with a line on diagram).

Row 1 (WS): Sl 1 pwise, knit to end of row.

Row 2 (RS): Sl 1 kwise, knit to end of row.

Rep Rows 1-2 until there are 6 ridges on RS after a WS row. Now join right shoulder to corresponding piece on right front with Kitchener st—or, BO and seam with mattress st.

RIGHT SHOULDER

With charcoal and larger circular,

pick up and knit 51 sts, beginning at line on diagram: pick up and knit 6 sts along Staircase 13, Step 1, and then 11 sts along each of next 4 staircases, and 1 st in corner. Continue as for left shoulder.

FINISHING

BACK EDGING

Work as for Garter Stitch Edging with 2 Edge Stitches (without fold) on page 181.

Ridges

Pick Up and Knit Row:

Beginning at lower left corner of back, with charcoal and smaller circular, pick up and knit 140 sts along back: 1 st in corner, 11 sts along each staircase, 6 sts along back band, 11 sts along each staircase, and 1 st in corner. Knit 1 row.

Garter Stitch Edging with 2 Edge Stitches

K-CO 7 sts as an extension of last row and work edging, using dpn to help. BO when only 7 sts rem.

EDGINGS ALONG FRONTS AND FRONT AND BACK NECK

Work as for Garter Stitch Edging with 2 Edge Stitches (page 181). The corners are explained in more detail later in the pattern.

Ridges

Row 1 (RS), pick up and knit row: With charcoal and smaller long circular, pick up and knit sts, beginning at lower right front with 1 st in corner at Staircase 1,

Step 1, 11 sts along each of the 6 staircases and 1 st in corner, 6 sts along lowest staircase, 11 sts along the next 8 staircases, 1 st in corner at front neck, 11 + 6 sts on front neck, 1 st in corner, 5 sts along shoulder, 1 st in corner, 6 + 11 + 6 + 11 sts on back neck, 1 st in corner, 5 sts along shoulder, 1 st in corner at front neck, 6 + 11 sts on front neck, 1 st in corner, 11 sts along the 8 staircases, 6 sts along lowest staircase, 1 st in corner, 11 sts along each staircase on lower right back, and 1 st in corner. Pm between sts for each buttonhole (see arrows on diagram).

Row 2 (WS): Knit.

There is now 1 ridge on RS.

Garter Stitch Edging with 2 Edge Stitches

K-CO 7 sts as an extension of last row. Work edging all around and work 4 buttonholes on right front at markers.

Buttonholes

Work on RS: Sl 2 pwise, k1, BO 3 sts, slip st back to left needle, p2tog, slip st to left needle, K-CO 3 sts; turn, knit to end of row.

Corner

Turn corners with German short rows (DS), see page 186.

Row 1 (RS): Sl 2 pwise, k4; turn.

Row 2 (WS): DS (= sl 1 pwise, pulling up on working yarn to flip st upside down so it has 2 legs on needle—do not knit st), knit to end of row; turn.

Row 3: Sl 2 pwise, k3; turn.

Row 4: DS, knit to end of row; turn.

Row 5: Sl 2 pwise, k2; turn.

Row 6: DS, knit to end of row; turn.

Row 7: Sl 2 pwise, k1; turn.

Row 8: DS, knit to end of row (= k1); turn.

Row 9: Sl 2 pwise, knit the 2 legs of DS tog as one; turn.

Row 10: Knit to end of row; turn.

Row 11: Sl 2 pwise, k1, knit the 2 legs of DS tog as one; turn.

Row 12: Knit to end of row; turn.

Row 13: Sl 2 pwise, k2, knit the 2 legs of DS tog as one; turn.

Row 14: Knit to end of row; turn.

Row 15: Sl 2 pwise, k3, knit the 2 legs of DS tog as one; turn.

Row 16: Knit to end of row; turn. BO.

Sew buttons on left front opposite buttonholes.

FINISHING

Measure across half of top of one sleeve, and measure that length from center of one shoulder down, respectively, on back and front and pm. The relation is 1 st from sleeve to 1 ridge on back/front.

Attach each sleeve between markers. Seam each sleeve from the top down. Seam sides.

6
ZIGZAG

ZIGZAG

SCHOOL 6

Downward staircases become a horizontal zigzag pattern. Zigzag staircases are entertaining to knit. They are alternately knitted and purled, with each staircase consisting of steps that form rectangles, ending and beginning with cropped figures.

FINISHED MEASUREMENTS
Whole Swatch: 6¾ x 6¾ in / 17x 17 cm
Single Zigzag: 1 step wide and 2 steps high, approx. 2 x 2 in / 5 x 5 cm

MATERIALS
Yarn: CYCA #3 (DK, light worsted) Filcolana Pernilla (100% pure new wool, 191 yd/175 m / 50 g)
Yarn Colors and Amounts:
Willow Heather 822 (khaki)
Charcoal Heather 956 (charcoal)
Acacia Heather 825 (curry)

Needles: U. S. size 2.5 / 3 mm: 2 dpn and 16 in / 40 cm circular

SWATCH
Diagram
The diagram on page 114 shows all staircases and steps.

Stitches and Ridges
A step can have any even number of stitches. The number of ridges should be half the stitch count of the step.
This pattern includes 3 sizes of staircases: 12 sts and 6 ridges for the swatch (16 sts and 8 ridges for the Zigzag Poncho, 20 sts and 10 ridges for the Zigzag Vest). Each step in the swatch has 12 sts and 6 ridges.

Rule of Thumb
Always begin a staircase where the last-knitted one ended. The yarn should always hang at outer edge at the last-knitted stitch, ready to be the beginning stitch for the next staircase.

STAIRCASE 1
Purl with **khaki** from left to right.

Step 1
Purl beginning step—a rectangle. K-CO 12 (16, 20) sts with 2 beg sts. Begin with dpn and change to circular when comfortable.
Row 1 (WS): Purl. There is now 1 ridge on RS.
Row 2 (WS): Sl 1 kwise, purl to end of row.
Row 3: Sl 1 kwise, purl to end of row.
Row 4: Sl 1 kwise, purl to end of row.
There are now 2 ridges on both RS and WS.
Rep Rows 3-4 until there are 6 (8, 10) ridges on both RS and WS (photo A). The last row is on WS. When RS faces you, the yarn end is at left side and working yarn on right. Pm on RS.

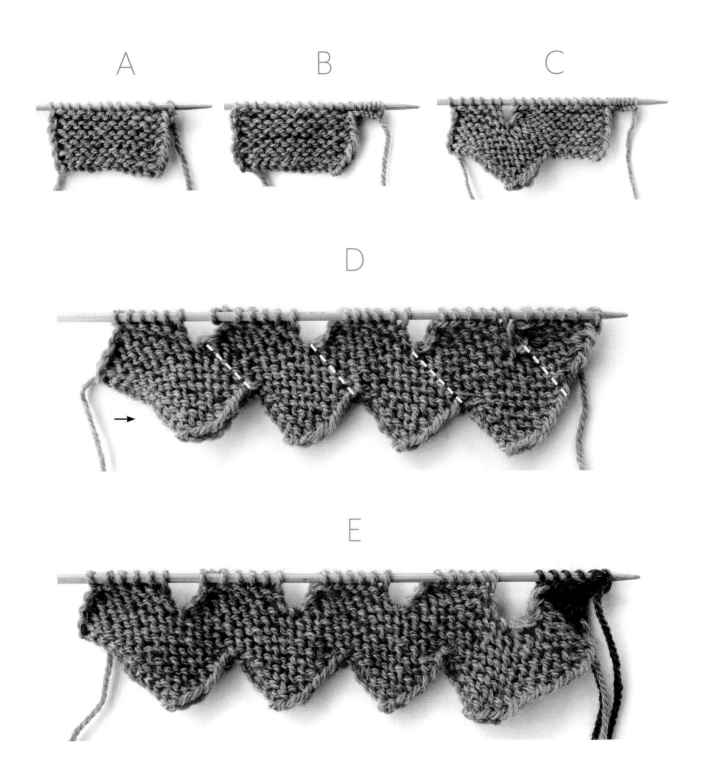

F

G

H   I

Step 2
Purl intermediate step—a rectangle.

Holding Step 1 in your left hand with RS facing you, K-CO 6 (8, 10) sts as an extension of Step 1's sts = 18 (24, 30) sts (photo B).

Row 1 (RS): *P12 (16, 20); turn. There is now 1 ridge on RS.*

Continue over these 12 (16, 20) sts, leaving rem 6 (8, 10) sts to rest.

Row 2 (WS): *Sl 1 kwise, purl to end of row = p11 (15, 19).*

Row 3 (RS): *Sl 1 kwise, purl to end of row = p11 (15, 19).*

Rep Rows 2-3 until there are 6 (8, 10) ridges on both RS and WS (photo C).

Steps 3 and 4
Purl intermediate steps— rectangles.

Work as for Step 2.

Step 5
Purl end step—a square.

Row 1 (RS): *Sl 1 kwise, p5 (7, 9); turn. There is now 1 ridge on RS.*

Continue over these 6 (8, 10) sts, leaving rem 6 (8, 10) sts to rest.

Row 2 (WS): *Sl 1 kwise, purl to end of row.*

Row 3 (RS): *Sl 1 kwise, purl to end of row.*

Rep Rows 2-3 until there are 6 (8, 10) ridges on both RS and WS = 12 (16, 20) total (photo D). Cut yarn.

STAIRCASE 2
Knit with **charcoal** from right to left.

Begin where last staircase ended.

Step 1
Knit beginning step—a triangle.

Row (RS): Sl 1 kwise, p1; turn.

Row 2 (WS): Sl 1 kwise, k1.

Row 3: Sl 1 pwise, M1, p2tog (with 1 charcoal and 1 khaki st); turn.

Row 4: Sl 1 kwise, knit to end of row.

Row 5: Sl 1 pwise, M1, k1, p2tog; turn.

Row 6: Sl 1 kwise, knit to end of row.

Row 7: Sl 1 pwise, M1, knit to last charcoal st, p2tog; turn.

Rep Rows 6-7 until there are 6 (8, 10) charcoal sts (photo E). End with a WS row.

Step 2
Knit intermediate step—a rectangle.

Row 1 (RS): Sl 1 pwise, k5 (7, 9), pick up and knit 7 (9, 11) sts along the top side of staircase below: pick up and knit 1 st for every ridge; move last-knitted st to left needle and p2tog = 13 (17, 21) sts; turn.

Row 2 (WS): Sl 1 kwise, k5 (7, 9), k2tog, knit to end of row = 12 (16, 20) sts.

Row 3: Sl 1 pwise, knit to last charcoal st, p2tog (joining 1 charcoal and 1 khaki st); turn.

Row 4: Sl 1 kwise, knit to end of row.

Rep Rows 3-4 until all the khaki sts have been eliminated and there are 6 (8, 10) ridges on RS (photo F). The last row is on WS.

Step 3
Knit intermediate step—a rectangle.

Row 1 (RS): Sl 1 pwise, k11 (15, 19), pick up and knit 7 (9, 11) sts along the top side of staircase below: pick up and knit 1 st for every ridge; move last-knitted st to left needle and p2tog = 19 (25, 31 sts; turn.

Row 2 (WS): Sl 1 kwise, k5 (7, 9), k2tog, k5 (7, 9) = 12 (16, 20) sts; turn.

Row 3: Sl 1 pwise, k10 (14, 18), p2tog (joining 1 charcoal and 1 khaki st); turn.

Row 4: Sl 1 kwise, knit to end of row.

Rep Rows 3-4 until there are 6 (8, 10) ridges on RS and 5 (7, 9) ridges on WS. The last row is on WS.

Steps 4 and 5
Knit intermediate step— rectangles.

Work as for Step 3.

Step 6
Knit end step—a cropped rectangle.

Row 1 (RS): Sl 1 pwise, k11 (15, 19), pick up and knit 7 (9, 11) sts along edge sts of last step of staircase below = 19 (25, 31 sts; turn.

Row 2 (WS): Sl 1 pwise, k5 (7, 9), k2tog, k5 (7, 9); turn. Leave last 6 (8, 10) sts on needle to rest.

Row 3: Sl 1 pwise, knit until 3 sts rem, k2tog, k1.

Row 4: Sl 1 pwise, knit to end of row.

Rep Rows 3-4 until there are 6 (8, 10) sts and 6 (8, 10) ridges on RS. The last row is on RS (photo G). Cut yarn.

Photo H shows Staircases 1 and 2 on WS.

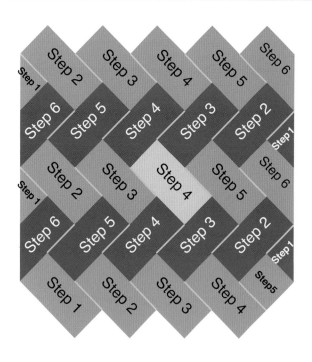

DIAGRAM FOR SCHOOL 6

■ Charcoal
■ Khaki
□ Curry

STAIRCASE 3

Purl with **khaki** *from left to right. Begin where last staircase ended (here, Staircase 2).*

Step 1

Purl beginning step*—a triangle.*
Row 1 (WS): *Sl 1 pwise, k1; turn.*
Row 2 (RS): *Sl 1 pwise, p1; turn.*
Row 3: *Sl 1 kwise, M1, sl 1, k1, psso (with 1 khaki and 1 charcoal); turn.*
Row 4: *Sl 1 pwise, p2; turn.*
Row 5: *Sl 1 kwise, M1, p1, sl 1, k1, psso; turn.*
Row 6: *Sl 1 pwise, p3; turn.*
Row 7: *Sl 1 kwise, M1, purl to last khaki st (here: p2), sl 1, k1, psso; turn.*
Row 8: *Sl 1 pwise, purl to end of row; turn.*
Rep Rows 7-8 until there are 7 (8, 10) khaki sts (photo 1). End on a RS row.

Step 2

Purl intermediate step*—a rectangle.*
Row 1 (WS): *Sl 1 kwise, p5 (7, 9), pick up and purl 7 (9, 11) sts along top of staircase below: 1 st for every ridge = 13 (17, 21) sts; move last worked st to left needle under yarn, move yarn back over to right needle before st between the 2 needles and work sl 1, k1, psso wyun; turn.*
Row 2 (RS): *Sl 1 pwise, p5 (7, 9), p2tog, purl to end of row = 12 (16, 20) sts.*
Row 3: *Sl 1 kwise, p10 (14, 18), sl 1, k1, psso.*
Row 4: *Sl 1 pwise, purl to end of row. Rep Rows 3-4 until there are 6 (8, 10) ridges on RS and 5 (7, 9) ridges on WS. The last row is on RS.*

Step 3

Purl intermediate step*—a rectangle.*
Row 1 (WS): *Sl 1 kwise, p11 (15, 19), pick up and purl 7 (9, 11) sts along top of staircase below: 1 st for every ridge = 19 (25, 31) sts; move last worked st to left needle under yarn, move yarn back over to right needle before st between the 2 needles and work sl 1, k1, psso wyun; turn.*
Continue as for Step 2, beginning on Row 2.

Step 4

Purl intermediate step*—a rectangle.*
Work as for Step 3, working first 6 (8, 10) sts with khaki and rest of step with curry.

Step 5

Purl intermediate step—*a rectangle after contrast-color step.*
Work as for Step 3, working first 6 (8, 10) sts with curry and rest of step with khaki.

Step 6

Purl end step—*cropped rectangle.*
Row 1 (WS): *Sl 1 kwise, p11 (15, 19), pick up and purl 7 (9, 11) sts in the charcoal edge sts = 19 (25, 31) sts; turn.*
Row 2 (RS): *Sl 1 kwise, p5 (7, 9), p2tog, p5 (7, 9). Turn, leaving last 6 (8, 10) sts on needle to rest.*
Row 3: *Sl 1 kwise, purl to last 3 sts, p2tog, p1; turn.*
Row 4: *Sl 1 kwise, purl to end of row.*
Rep Rows 3-4 until there are 6 (8, 10) ridges and 6 (8, 10) sts. The last row is on WS. Cut yarn.

STAIRCASE 4

Knit with **charcoal** from right to left and as for Staircase 2. Begin where last staircase ended.

STAIRCASE 5

Purl with **khaki** *from left to right and as for Staircase 3. Begin where last staircase ended.*

FINISHING

Begin where purl staircase ended. BO the first 5 sts with khaki, *pick up and knit 1 st after each ridge (6 total, the bind-off ridge is not included) in step's left side, and BO them—*at the same time, BO next step's sts pwise (6 total)*. Rep * to * until all "sawtooth" edges have been bound off. Weave in all ends.

ZIGZAG VEST

Pretty, soft, and downy—everything lovely in one package. The zigzag staircases are worked alternately with Silk Mohair and Tvinni, an elegant combination. Wear it next to your skin or with a T-shirt or blouse underneath. The back and front are worked in one long piece. Doubled edges frame the sides with buttons sewn on through both layers. The neckline is edged with a fine I-cord bind-off.

SIZE
Medium

FINISHED MEASUREMENTS
Chest: 39½ in / 100 cm
Total Length: 19¾ in / 50 cm

MATERIALS
Yarn: CYCA #2 (sport) Isager Tvinni (100% pure new Merino wool, 279 yd/255 m / 50 g)
Yarn Colors and Amounts:
Color A: Ice-Blue Heather 10s: 50 g
Color C: Light Lime 29s: 50 g
Color E: Ice Blue 10: 50 g

Yarn: CYCA #0 (lace) Isager Silk Mohair (75% kid mohair, 25% mulberry silk, 232 yd/212 m / 25 g)
Yarn Colors and Amounts:
Color B: Mint 66: 25 g
Color D: Blue 41: 25 g
Color G: Dark Mint 67: 25 g

Needles: U. S. size 1.5 / 2.5 mm: 2 dpn and 24 in / 60 cm circular
U. S. size 2.5 / 3 mm: 1 dpn

Notions: 8 small buttons

GAUGE
25 sts and 56 rows/28 ridges in garter st with Tvinni on U. S. 1.5 / 2.5 mm needles = 4 x 4 in / 10 x 10 cm.
24 sts and 52 rows/26 ridges in garter st with Silk Mohair on U. S. 1.5 / 2.5 mm needles = 4 x 4 in / 10 x 10 cm.
1 step of 20 sts and 10 ridges on RS is 5 in / 12.5 cm wide and 2½ in / 6 cm long.
2 steps measured diagonally = 4 in / 10 cm.
Adjust needle size to obtain correct gauge if necessary.

INSTRUCTIONS

Technique
The pattern is based on School 6 (page 114), with steps in 3 sizes. Learn the technique by working the whole School 6 swatch.

Diagram
Follow the diagram on page 122, which shows the color sequence, direction of working, staircases, and steps—or follow the instructions for the largest size for the School 6 swatch.

Stitches and Ridges
Each step has 20 sts and 10 ridges on RS.

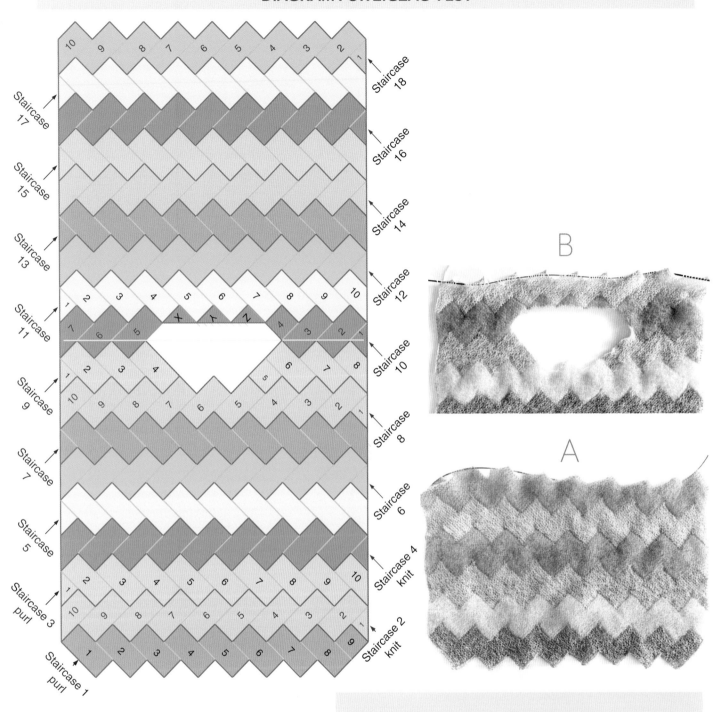

Color A: Ice-Blue Heather Tvinni
Color B: Mint Silk Mohair
Color C: Light Lime Tvinni
Color D: Blue Silk Mohair
Color E: Ice-Blue Tvinni
Color G: Dark Mint Silk Mohair

Direction of Knitting/Purling for Staircases

Purl staircases = odd-numbered, with **black** numbers and worked from left to right.

Knit staircases = even-numbered, with **red** numbers and worked from right to left.

Always begin a staircase where the last one ended.

BACK AND FRONT

STAIRCASE 1

*This staircase is **purled** with Color A as for School 6, Staircase 1, although this staircase is longer because it has more intermediate steps (as Step 2). There are now 90 sts on needle.*

STAIRCASE 2

This staircase is **knitted** with Color B as for School 6, Staircase 2, although this staircase is longer because it has more intermediate steps (as Step 2).

STAIRCASE 3

*This staircase is **purled** and single color with Color C as for School 6, Staircase 3, although this staircase is longer because it has more intermediate steps (as step 2).*

STAIRCASES 4, 5, 6, AND 7

Worked in colors shown on diagram (photo A shows Staircases 1 to 6). Work Staircases 4 and 6 as for Staircase 2. *Work Staircases 5 and 7 as for Staircase 3.*

Marking front neck at Staircases 8, 9, and 10

Pink lines show where you will end with stitches placed on a holder for later. **Green** lines show that stitches are cast on here. **Black** lines show that there is a side with edge stitches here.

STAIRCASE 8

Work as for Staircase 2 and in same color, but place the 10 sts on right side of Steps 5 and 6 on a holder for later.

STAIRCASE 9
Steps 1, 2, 3, and 4

Work as for Staircase 3, Steps 1, 2, 3, and 4. End Step 4 by placing all 20 sts on a holder to leave space for the front neck.

Step 5

First step after front neck opening—a square.

Row 1 (WS), pick up and purl: *Pick up and purl 10 sts along Step 5's short side: 1 st in edge st after each ridge, k1, pass 1ˢᵗ st over 2ⁿᵈ; turn.*

Row 2 (RS): *Sl 1 pwise, purl to end of row (= 10 sts).*

Row 3: *Sl 1 kwise, p8, sl 1, k1, psso; turn.*

Row 4: *Sl 1 pwise, purl to end of row. Rep Rows 3-4 until there are 10 ridges on RS. The last row is on RS.*

Steps 6, 7, and 8

Work as for Staircase 3, Steps 8, 9, and 10.

STAIRCASE 10
Steps 1, 2, and 3

Knit with Color D as for Staircase 2, Steps 1, 2, and 3.

Step 4

Knit end step—a square.
Row 1 (RS), beginning row: Sl 1 kwise, purl to end of row (= 20 sts).

Row 2 (WS): Sl 1 kwise, p9; turn.
Row 3 (RS): Sl 1 pwise, p9; turn.
Rep Rows 2-3 until there are 10 ridges on RS. The last row is on RS.

Cut yarn.
There is space for front neck opening after Step 4. Triangles X, Y, and Z are worked last.

Step 5

Turn work so WS faces you. With Color D, K-CO 11 sts as part of row, where Staircase 9, Step 4 ended. Turn so RS faces you and continue by picking up and knitting 10 sts along Staircase 9, Step 4's free short side. Work a rectangle here (as for School 6, Staircase 2, Step 3).

Steps 6 and 7

Work as for Staircase 2, Steps 9 and 10.

STAIRCASE 11

This staircase looks completely normal, but it is different from the other purl staircases (photo B).

Steps 1, 2, and 3

Work as for Staircase 3, Steps 1, 2, and 3.

Step 4

Continue as for Step 3 (or as for Staircase 1, Step 2), and k1 in corner loop of last st of pick up and knit row. The step ends on right side toward front neck (as on Staircase 1); K-CO 10 sts as an extension of previous row.

Steps 5 and 6

Work as for Staircase 1, Step 2.

Step 7

Step 7 is worked together with the 10 sts from Staircase 10, Step 4.

Row 1 (RS): *Sl 1 kwise, purl to end of row; turn and K-CO 11 sts; turn again, and knit first st of Staircase 10, Step 4, pass knit st over last st cast on; turn.*

Row 2 (WS): *Sl 1 pwise, p9, p2tog, p9; turn, leaving last 10 sts on needle.*

Row 3: *Sl 1 kwise, p18, sl 1, k1, psso; turn.*

Row 4: *Sl 1 pwise, p19; turn.*

Rep Rows 3-4 until there are 10 ridges on RS.

The last row is on RS.

Steps 8, 9, and 10

Work as for Staircase 3, Steps 8, 9, and 10.

STAIRCASES 12, 14, AND 16

Work as for Staircase 2.

STAIRCASES 13, 15, AND 17

Work as for Staircase 3.

STAIRCASE 18

Work as for Staircase 2. Do not cut yarn.

FINISHING ON BODY

Begin where Staircase 18 ended and turn with WS facing you. BO the first 9 sts along Step 10, *pick up and knit 1 st in edge st before the first ridge and pick up and knit 1 st in edge st after each of the

following ridges (= 11 sts) on left side of step, and *at the same time* BO sts of next step (= 10 sts)*. Rep from * to * until you've bound off along all 9 "sawteeth." Cut yarn and weave in all ends.

FINISHING
BACK NECK TRIANGLES ALONG STAIRCASE 11

Use Color D and 2 dpn U. S. 1.5 / 2.5 mm. Turn chart upside down and work Triangles X, Y, and Z in the notches along Staircase 11 (photo B) as follows:

TRIANGLE X

Pick up and knit 1 st between Colors D and E (Staircase 10, Step 5 and Staircase 11, Step 4), and then 10 sts along Staircase 11, Step 4 (= 11 sts). Place the 10 cast-on loops from Step 5 on the other needle and end by placing corner loop on needle (= 11 sts).
Place the last-knitted st on left needle and p2tog; turn.
Row 1 (WS): Sl 1 pwise, knit to end of row; turn.
Row 2 (RS): Sl 1 pwise, k2tog, knit to last st (here: 7 sts) with Color D, p2tog (last st with Color D together with first cast-on loop); turn.
Row 3 (WS): Sl 1 kwise, knit to end of row; turn.
Rep Rows 2-3 until there are 3 sts with Color E and 4 sts with Color D after a WS row.
Next Row (RS): Sl 1 pwise, k2tog, p2tog; turn.

Next Row (WS): Sl 1 kwise, k2; turn.
Next Row (RS): Sl 1, k1, psso, p2tog; turn.
Next Row (WS): Sl 1 kwise, k1; turn.
Next Row (RS): Sl 1 pwise, p2tog, pass slipped st over p2tog (= 1 st) rem.

TRIANGLE Y

Use last st of Triangle X, and pick up and knit 10 sts along Step 5 and place the 10 cast-on loops of Step 6 on other needle. Work as for Triangle X.

TRIANGLE Z

Use last st of Triangle Y, and pick up and knit 10 sts along Step 6 and place the 10 cast-on loops of Step 7 on other needle. Work as for Triangle X.

NECKBAND

Place held sts of front (pink lines) on circular U.S. 1.5 / 2.5 mm and, with Color E, pick up and knit sts around front neck, beginning at back neck: 11 sts along Staircase 10, Step 5 (green line), 11 sts each along Triangles X, Y and Z, 11 sts along Step 4 (black line), and, continuing on front: 20 sts along Staircase 9, Steps 6 and 5 (black line), k10 along Step 5 (pink line), 1 st between 5 and 6, pick up and knit 10 sts along right side of 6 (black line), k10 along left side of Step 6 (pink line), 1 st between 6 and 7, 10 sts along 7 (black line),

and k20 along Staircase 9, Step 4 (pink line) = 137 sts.
BO with I-cord bind-off:

I-Cord BO

K-CO 2 sts onto left needle tip where round began.
With circular in left hand and using U. S. 2.5 / 3 mm dpn to help in right hand.
Row 1 (RS): K1, sl 1, k1, psso.
Place the 2 sts back on circular. Rep Row 1.
Make sure the bind-off is not too tight. If so, use a larger dpn. Before sts between Staircase 8, Steps 5 and 6, and between 6 and 7 (at base of notches), k1, p2tog, pass slipped st over joined st **while** in top of 6 (center front), k2, slip sts back to left needle and continue as est.
When all but 2 sts have been bound off, BO these sts. Join rem 2 sts to 2 cast-on sts to splice cord.

EDGING ON RIGHT SIDE Ridges
Row 1 (RS), pick up and knit:
Begin at Staircase 18 directly over ending. With Color E and 24 in / 60 cm circular U. S. 1.5 / 2.5 mm,

1 Increase in Edge Stitch

First work 1 st in top loop of edge stitch, and then 1 st under both loops.

pick up and knit sts: 13 sts per
staircase (with 1 increase in
edge st in some of edge sts) =
221 sts.
Row 2 (WS): Sl 1 pwise, k2tog,
knit to end of row.

Garter Stitch Edging with 1 Edge Stitch

Change to Color E and K-CO
5 sts as extension of sts on
needle.

With circular in one hand and
dpn in the other.
Row 1 (RS): K4, p2tog; turn.
Row 2 (WS): Sl 1 kwise, knit
to end of row.
Row 3 (RS): Sl 1 pwise, k3,
p2tog; turn.
Rep Rows 2-3 until 5 sts rem.
BO.

EDGING ON LEFT SIDE

Work as for edging on right
side, but begin at lower left
side of front, at Staircase 2.

Arrange vest so edging on
front overlaps edging on back,
making front slightly longer
than back. Sew on 4 buttons
through both layers at each
side.

ZIGZAG PONCHO

The poncho on these pages is large, cozy, and pretty in so many ways. Add a belt on the back or front, or simply arrange the front pieces around your neck and shoulders. For yet another option, sew on some snap closures and wear it as a vest.

SIZE
One size

FINISHED MEASUREMENTS
Width: across back without edging, 29¼ in / 74 cm
Length: at center back from tip to back neck, 34¼ in / 87 cm; from tip at center back to right/left side, 19 in / 48 cm
Edging: 1 in / 2.5 cm

MATERIALS
Yarn: CYCA #2 (sport) Isager Tweed (70% wool, 30% mohair, 219 yd/200 m / 50 g)
Yarn Colors and Amounts:
Bottle Green (dark green): 250 g
Lime: 150 g
Turquoise: 100 g

Needles: U. S. size 1.5 / 2.5 mm: 2 dpn + 24, 32, and 48 in / 60, 80, and 120 cm circulars

Notions: snaps (optional)

GAUGE
25 sts and 52 rows/26 ridges in garter st = 4 x 4 in / 10 x 10 cm.
1 step = approx. 1¼ in / 3 cm in height and 2½ in / 6 cm in width. Adjust needle size to obtain correct gauge if necessary.

INSTRUCTIONS

Technique
The poncho is a combination of the staircases in Schools 5 and 6 (pp. 90 and 110) as well as the diagram on page 126. Learn the technique by working the School 5 swatch, or just the first 4 staircases using the yarn you'll knit with for the poncho. You can measure the gauge from the beginning sections of the poncho.

Diagram
Turn the diagram so the text is right side up and can easily be read (horizontal). Or, go to School 5, work up through the Staircase 8, and then continue following School 6. The stitch count is the same as the middle size in School 6.

Stitches and Ridges
Each step has 16 sts and 8 ridges.

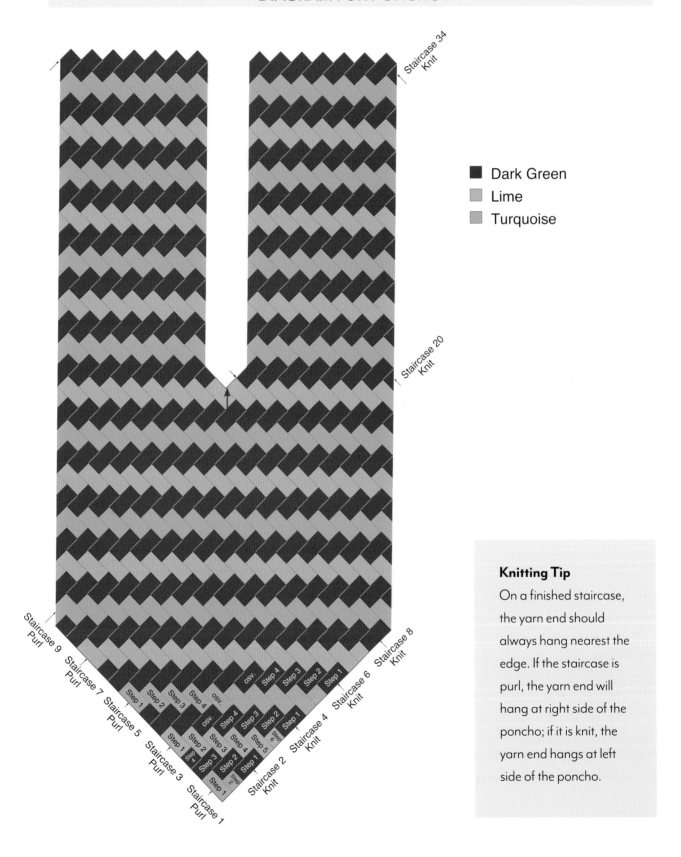

Dark Green
Lime
Turquoise

Knitting Tip

On a finished staircase, the yarn end should always hang nearest the edge. If the staircase is purl, the yarn end will hang at right side of the poncho; if it is knit, the yarn end hangs at left side of the poncho.

BACK

Begin with dpn and then change to longer and longer circulars as necessary. Work back and forth for the rest of the poncho.

STAIRCASES 1, 2, 3, AND 4

Work as for first 4 staircases of School 5 with the following color sequence: Staircase 1: turquoise, Staircase 2: dark green, Staircase 3: lime, and Staircase 4: dark green.

These 4 staircases form bottom tip on diagram.

STAIRCASE 5

Purl with turquoise.

Work as for School 5, Staircase 3, but single-color and longer.

STAIRCASES 6 TO 8

Continue in color sequence. After 8 staircases, the tip is compete.

STAIRCASE 9

*This is a **purl** staircase with turquoise and worked as for School 6, Staircase 3, but longer.*

It is the first straight staircase that begins and ends with a diagonal step. It is worked with turquoise; the later purl staircases are alternately worked with turquoise and lime.

Step 1

Purl beginning step—a triangle.

Hold piece with WS facing you.

Row 1 (WS): *With turquoise, K-CO 1 st beginning in previous dark green st. Sl 1 kwise, sl 1, k1, psso (see page 172); turn.*

Row 2 (RS): *Sl 1 pwise, p1; turn.*

Row 3: *Sl 1 kwise, 1 e-inc, sl 1, k1, psso (3 turquoise sts); turn.*

Row 4: *Sl 1 pwise, p2; turn.*

Row 5: *Sl 1 kwise, 1 e-inc, p1, sl 1, k1, psso (4 turquoise sts); turn.*

Row 6 and all following RS rows: *Sl 1 pwise, purl to end of row; turn.*

Row 7: *Sl 1 kwise, 1 e-inc, p2, sl 1, k1, psso (5 turquoise sts); turn.*

Row 9: *Sl 1 kwise, 1 e-inc, p3, sl 1, k1, psso (6 turquoise sts); turn.*

Row 11: *Sl 1 kwise, 1 e-inc, p4, sl 1, k1, psso (7 turquoise sts); turn.*

Row 13: *Sl 1 kwise, 1 e-inc, p5, sl 1, k1, psso (8 turquoise sts); turn.*

End at left side after a RS row.

Steps 2-16

Purl intermediate steps—rectangles. Continue as for School 6, Staircase 3, Step 2. After Row 1, there are 17 sts on needle.

Step 17

Purl end step—a cropped step. Work as for School 6, Staircase 3, Step 6. The last step of staircase is a cropped step.

Row 1 (WS): *Sl 1 kwise, p15, pick up and purl 1 st between turquoise and dark green, and then p8 = 25 sts; turn.*

Row 2 (RS): *Sl 1 kwise, p2tog, p5, p2tog, p7 = 15 sts. Leave last 8 sts on needle to rest; turn.*

Row 3: *Sl 1 kwise, purl to end of row; turn.*

Row 4: *Sl 1 kwise, p2tog, purl to end of row; turn.*

Rep Rows 3-4 with fewer and fewer sts until 8 sts rem and there are 8 ridges on RS.

The last row is a WS row. Cut yarn.

STAIRCASE 10

Knit this staircase with dark green as for School 6, Staircase 2.

STAIRCASES 11 TO 19

Work as for Staircases 9 and 10 alternately, in colors following diagram.

RIGHT FRONT

Continue straight up on right side of poncho.

STAIRCASE 20

Knit with dark green.

Steps 1 to 8

Work as for Staircase 10 of back, Steps 1-8.

Place last 8 sts towards center on a holder. Also place sts of left front on a holder.

STAIRCASE 21

Purl with turquoise.

Steps 1 to 7

Work as for Staircase 9 of back, Steps 1-7.

Step 8

Work Step 8 as for Staircase 10 of back, Step 17.

STAIRCASES 22 TO 34

Continue up.

FINISHING

Turn work with RS facing you and, with dark green, pick up and knit 8 sts along right side of first point (Step 2's right side) and, *at the same time,* BO. *continue to BO

7 sts, pick up and knit 8 sts along right side of next step and BO *at the same time**; rep * to * until all sts have been bound off and all points have been finished off.

LEFT FRONT
Continue straight up on left side of poncho.

STAIRCASE 20
Knit with dark green.

Place held sts on circular except for the 8 sts nearest center that were placed on holder. Work as for Staircase 6 but begin with half step (8 sts) and end as for earlier dark green steps.

STAIRCASES 21 to 34
Work as for corresponding staircase on right front.

FINISHING
Work to match edge on right front.

EDGINGS

The edgings along the inner and outer sides are worked as for the Garter Stitch Edging with 2 Edge Stitches, page 181; here, with 8 stitches.

INNER SIDE OF LEFT FRONT
Ridges
Row 1 (RS), pick up and knit:
Begin between Staircases 19 and 20 at the black arrow, (see also photo A) and, with dark green and 32 in / 80 cm circular, pick up and knit 1 st between dark green and lime and 8 sts in edge sts along the lime pieces towards center back (red arrow). Place the 8 held sts onto dpn and knit them, pick up and knit 1 st between lime and dark green, 8 sts along dark green (Staircase 20), and then 9 sts along each of the following staircases until you've picked up sts along Staircase 34.
Row 2 (WS): Sl 1 pwise, knit to end of row.

Garter Edging with 2 Edge Stitches
Now work the edging on the diagonals of the vertical sts, using a dpn to help if necessary.
Row 1 (RS): Sl 2 pwise, k5, p2tog; turn.
Row 2 (WS): Sl 2 kwise, k6; turn.
Rep Rows 1-2 until 9 sts rem (1 vertical st and 8 sts of edge). The last row is on WS. BO, beginning with sl 1, k1 psso and ending with p2tog.

A

INNER SIDE OF RIGHT FRONT
Ridges
Row 1 (RS), pick up and knit:
Begin at Staircase 34 and, with dark green, pick up and knit 9 sts along each staircase. Place the 8 held sts of Staircase 20 onto dpn and knit them. Turn the already-knitted edge out and pick up and knit 8 sts in the lime edge sts toward center back in the lime notch behind the already-worked edge.

1 Increase in Edge Stitch
Work first st in top loop of edge st, and then work 1 stitch under both loops.

Row 2 (WS): Sl 1 pwise, knit to end of row.
End with K-CO 8 sts.

Garter Edging with 2 Edge Stitches
Row 1 (RS): K7, p2tog; turn.
Row 2 (WS): Sl 1 kwise, k7; turn.
Row 3 (RS): Sl 2 pwise, k5, p2tog; turn.
Rep Rows 2-3 and BO when 8 sts rem. The last row is on WS.

OUTER SIDE
Ridges
Row 1 (RS), pick up and knit:
Begin at lower edge of left front (top left on diagram) at arrow, and with dark green and longest circular, pick up and knit 9 sts along

B

each staircase to first corner on back (between Staircases 8 and 9).

Pm and then pick up and knit 16 sts per staircase (1 st per edge st/cast-on loop) to center back (at Staircase 1, Step 1), pm around this st. Pick up and knit 16 sts per staircase on third corner (between Staircases 8 and 9), and then 9 sts per staircase along right side until you've picked up sts along Staircase 34.

Row 2 (WS): Sl 1 pwise, knit to end of row.
End with K-CO 8 sts.

Garter Edging with 2 Edge Stitches

Row 1 (RS): P2, k5, p2tog; turn.

Row 2 (WS): Sl 1 kwise, k7; turn.
Row 3 (RS): Sl 2 pwise, k5, p2tog; turn.
Rep Rows 2–3. When first marker is reached, end on a WS row.

Corner on Left Side Between Staircases 8 and 9

Row 1 (RS): Sl 2 pwise, k1; turn.
Row 2 (WS): K1, p2tog; turn.
Row 3: K3; turn.
Row 4: Sl 2 pwise, k2; turn.
Row 5 and all following RS rows: Knit to end of row; turn.
Row 6: Sl 2 pwise, k3; turn.
Row 8: Sl 2 pwise, k4; turn.
Row 10: Sl 2 pwise, k5; turn.
Row 12: Sl 2 pwise, k5, p2tog; turn.
Continue edge as est before marker at center back point.

Center Back Point (photo B)

Use German short rows (DS) to turn corner; see page 186.
Row 1 (RS): Sl 2 pwise, k4; turn.
Row 2 (WS): DS (pull working yarn so st flips up and now has 2 legs), knit to end of row.
Row 3: Sl 2 pwise, k3; turn.
Row 4: DS, knit to end of row.
Row 5: Sl 2 pwise, k2; turn.
Row 6: DS, knit to end of row.
Row 7: Sl 2 pwise, k1; turn.
Row 8: DS, knit to end of row (= k1).
Row 9: Sl 2 pwise, knit both legs of DS as one st.
Row 10: Knit to end of row.
Row 11: Sl 2 pwise, k1, knit both legs of DS as one st; turn.
Row 12: Knit to end of row.
Row 13: Sl 2 pwise, k2, knit both legs of DS as one st; turn.
Row 14: Knit to end of row.
Row 15: Sl 2 pwise, k3, knit both legs of DS as one st; turn.
Row 16: Knit to end of row.

Corner on Right Side Between Staircases 8 and 9

Row 1 (RS): Sl 2 pwise, k5; turn.
Row 2 and all following WS rows: Knit to end of row; turn.
Row 3: Sl 2 pwise, k4; turn.
Row 5: Sl 2 pwise, k3; turn.
Row 7: Sl 2 pwise, k2; turn.
Row 9: Sl 2 pwise, k1; turn.
Row 11: Sl 2 pwise, k5, p2tog; turn.

Continue edging until all horizontal sts have been eliminated and only 8 sts rem. BO.

7

SHELLS

SHELLS

You'll learn how to knit shells in this school. The idea is "stolen" from a nineteenth-century baby blanket knitted with a fine white cotton yarn on very small needles. On the original blanket, the shells were knitted individually and joined last. This technique can be used for shawls, baby blankets, summer tops, etc. When the triangles are knitted together in diagonal panels, they look like shells, because they don't fit perfectly into the puzzle and so they bend into arches.

FINISHED MEASUREMENTS
Width: 10¾ in / 27 cm
Height: approx. 9½ in / 24 cm

MATERIALS
Yarn: Leftovers of a fine wool yarn
Yarn Colors and Amounts:
Yellow-Green: 50 g ball
Green: 50 g ball
Light Red: 10 g
Salmon: 10g

Needles: U. S. size 1.5 / 2.5 mm: dpn (or hybrid jumper needle), 24 in / 60 cm circular

Notions: Locking ring markers

GAUGE
1 shell = 2¾ x 5¼ in / 7 x 13 cm
Adjust needle size to obtain correct gauge if necessary.

SWATCH
Knit the swatch following pattern below and diagram.
One shell consists of a hill (in reverse stockinette) and a valley (stockinette) with 4 garter edge stitches on each side.

Stitch Count
A shell should always have an odd number of stitches, with the same number of stitches to either side of the center stitch.
The pattern has two sizes of shell:
Whole shells: 37 sts for the swatch (45 sts for the Wing Shawl).
Half shells: 19 sts for the swatch (23 sts for the Wing Shawl).

PANEL 1
Comprised of Shells 1 and 2.

Shell 1
This is the first shell, a beginning shell, which is the basis for the following shells.

Beginning Hill
Row 1 (RS), cast-on: With yellow-green and dpn, K-CO 37 (45) sts (with 2 beg sts).
Row 2 (WS): Sl 1 pwise, knit to end of row.
Row 3: Sl 1 pwise, p2, p2tog, purl to end of row.
Row 4: Sl 1 kwise, k2, k2tog, knit to last st, p1 = 35 (43) sts.

A Valley
Row 5 (RS): Sl 1 kwise, k2, k2tog, knit to end of row.
Row 6 (WS): Sl 1 pwise, k2, k2tog, purl until 4 sts rem, k4.
Row 7: Sl 1 pwise, k2, k2tog, knit to end of row.

A   B

Overview

Beginning shells: 1 and 3

Shell knitted between 2 shells: 5, 8, 9, 10, 13, and 14

Shell knitted between 2 shells with a joining stitch in the center: 4

Half shells, right half: 2, 6, and 11

Half shells, left half: 7, 12, and 16

Top shells: 15 and 17

DIAGRAM FOR SCHOOL 7

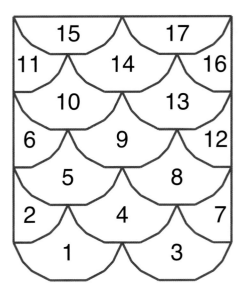

A Hill

Row 8 (WS): Sl 1 pwise, k2, k2tog, knit to end of row.

Row 9 (RS): Sl 1 pwise, k2, k2tog, purl until 4 sts rem, k4.

Row 10: Sl 1 pwise, k2, k2tog, knit to end of row.

Rep Rows 5-10 until 9 sts rem. End with a row on WS. Now work:
Sl 1 pwise, knit to end of row, but, k2tog at about the center of every row until 3 sts rem.
End with sl 1, k2tog, psso, place last st (= end st) on a locking marker and weave in ends (photo A).

Shell 2

A half shell (corresponds to the right half of a whole shell) with 19 (23) sts.

Beginning Hill

Knit with green.

Row 1 (RS), pick up and knit:
Beginning to left of end st, pick up and knit 18 (22) sts along top left of shell 1 and end with 1 st in the outermost left tip = 19 (23) sts.

Row 2 (WS): Sl 1 pwise, knit to end of row.

Row 3: Sl 1 pwise, p2, p2tog, purl to end of row = 18 (22) sts.

Row 4: Sl 1 kwise, knit to last st p1.

NOTE: There are **never** any decreases on WS. Mark the RS to keep track of which side of the shell you're working—it can be especially difficult to tell on larger pieces.

A Valley

Row 5 (RS): Sl 1 kwise, k2, k2tog, knit to end of row.

Row 6 (WS): Sl 1 pwise, k3, purl until 4 sts rem, k4.

Row 7: Sl 1 pwise, k2, k2tog, knit to end of row.

A Hill

Row 8 (WS): Sl 1 pwise, knit to end of row.

Row 9 (RS): Sl 1 pwise, k2, k2tog, purl until 4 sts rem, k4.

Row 10: Sl 1 pwise, knit to end of row.

Rep Rows 5-10 until 9 sts rem. End with a row on WS. Now work:

On WS: Sl 1 pwise, knit to end of row.

On RS: Sl 1 pwise, knit to end of row, but k2tog at about the center of row. When 3 sts rem, work next 4 rows as follows:

Next Row (WS): Sl 1 pwise, k2.

Next Row (RS): Sl 1 pwise, k2tog.

Next Row (WS): Sl 1 pwise, k1.

Next Row (RS): Sl 1, k1, psso. Place last st (= end st) on a locking marker and weave in ends.

PANEL 2

Comprised of Shells 3, 4, 5, and 6.

Shell 3

With yellow-green, work as for Shell 1.

Shell 4

With light red, work over Shells 3 and 1.

Row 1 (RS), pick up and knit:
Beginning to left of end st on Shell

Joining stitch
Place two shells (here: 3 and 1) with the end stitches pointing up and tip meeting tip (see diagram).
Join the corners as follows: Insert needle through the leftmost cast-on loop of Shell 3 and then through the rightmost cast-on loop of Shell 1, and knit them together, i.e. through both layers.

3, pick up and knit 18 (22) sts along top left of shell, knit 1 joining st (center st) and end with pick up and knit 18 (22) sts along right side of Shell 1; end right before marker = 37 (45) sts. Work as for Shell 1 from Row 2.

Shell 5

Row 1 (RS), pick up and knit:
Beginning to left of end st on Shell 4, pick up and knit 18 (22) sts along top left of shell, k1 in end st of shell 1 and end by picking up and knitting [18 (22) sts] along Shell 2 until just before end st = 37 (45) sts. Work as for Shell 2 from Row 2.

Shell 6

With green, work as for Shell 2 over Shell 5, but end pick-up-and-knit row with k1 in end st of Shell 2, and remove marker = 19 (23) sts. Work as for Shell 2 from Row 2.

PANEL 3
Shells 7 to 11.

Shell 7
This shell corresponds to the left half of a whole shell.
Work with green over Shell 3 along top right side.
Don't forget, **always** decrease on RS.

Beginning Hill
Knit with green.
Row 1 (RS), pick up and knit:
Pick up and knit 1 st in outer right corner and pick up and knit 18 (22) sts along top right side of Shell 3 = 19 (23) sts.
Row 2 (WS): Sl 1 pwise, knit to end of row.
Row 3: Sl 1 pwise, purl until 5 sts rem, p2tog, purl to end of row = 18 (22) sts.
Row 4: Sl 1 kwise, knit to last st p1.

A Valley
Row 5 (RS): Sl 1 kwise, knit until 5 sts rem, k2tog, knit to end of row.
Row 6 (WS): Sl 1 pwise, k3, purl until 4 sts rem, k4.
Row 7: Sl 1 pwise, knit until 5 sts rem, k2tog, knit to end of row.

A Hill
Row 8 (WS): Sl 1 pwise, knit to end of row.
Row 9 (RS): Sl 1 pwise, knit until 5 sts rem, k2tog, purl to end of row.
Row 10: Sl 1 pwise, knit to end of row.
Rep Rows 5-10 until 9 sts rem. End with a row on RS.
End as for Shell 2.

Work rest of panel as follows:
Shell 8 with yellow-green
Shell 9 with green
Shell 10 with yellow-green, as for Shells 4 and 5
Shell 11 with green, as for Shell 6

PANEL 4
Shells 12 to 15

Work Shell 12 with green as for Shell 7, but, work last st on pick-up-and-knit row in Shell 8's end st.

Work Shell 13 with salmon as for Shell 4.

Work Shell 14 with green as for Shell 5.

Shell 15
This shell is a top shell with yellow-green. It is worked "flat" on top with short rows.

A Hill
Row 1 (RS), pick up and knit:
With yellow-green, pick up and knit sts over shells 14, 10, and 11 as for rest of whole shells = 37 (45) sts.
Row 2 (WS): Sl 1 pwise, knit to end of row.
Row 3: Sl 1 pwise, purl until 2 sts rem; turn.
Row 4: Sl 1 kwise wyon, knit to last 2 sts; turn.

A Valley
Row 5 (RS): Sl 1 pwise, knit until 2 sts before previous turn; turn.
Row 6 (WS): Sl 1 pwise wyon, purl until 2 sts before previous turn; turn.

Row 7: Sl 1 kwise, knit until 2 sts before previous turn; turn.

A Hill
Row 8 (WS): Sl 1 pwise wyon, knit until 2 sts before previous turn; turn.
Row 9 (RS): Sl 1 pwise, purl until 2 sts before previous turn; turn.
Row 10: Sl 1 pwise wyon, knit until 2 sts before previous turn; turn.

Rep Rows 5-10 with fewer and fewer sts until 5 sts rem after turning and on a RS row.
Place all 37 (45) sts on a holder for later.

PANEL 5
Shells 16 and 17

Work Shell 16 with green as for Shell 12.

Work Shell 17 with yellow-green as for Shell 15.

There are now sts from 2 top shells and 3 sts on each locking ring marker.

TOP EDGING
Place all sts on 24 in / 60 cm circular, and with yellow-green:
Row 1 (RS): Knit.
Row 2 (WS): Sl 1 pwise wyon, knit to end of row.
Row 3: Sl 1 pwise wyon, purl to end of row.
Row 4: Sl 1 pwise wyon, knit to end of row.
BO.

WING SHAWL

A lavishly large shawl knitted with shells in downy-soft, super luxurious silk mohair yarn. It's just what you need to wrap up on a cool evening. The shawl consists of shells knitted in diagonal panels.

FINISHED MEASUREMENTS

Width: wingspan, 71 in / 180 cm

Length: measured at center of shawl from tip to long side, 30¼ in / 77 cm

MATERIALS

Yarn: CYCA #0 (lace) Hedgehog Fibres Kidsilk Lace (70% kid mohair, 30% silk, 459 yd/420 m / 50 g)

Yarn Colors and Amounts:
Fool's Gold (yellow): 250 g

Yarn: CYCA #0 (lace) Filcolana Tilia (70% superkid mohair, 30% mulberry silk, 230 yd/210 m / 25 g)

Yarn Colors and Amounts:
Begonia 322 (light red): 25 g
Peach Blossom 335 (salmon): 25 g
Purple 286 (gray-violet): 25 g

Needles: U. S. size 4 / 3.5 mm: 8 in / 20 cm hybrid jumper needle

U. S. size 2.5 / 3 mm: dpn (6 in / 15 cm) and 48 in / 120 cm circular

Notions: 1 stitch stopper

GAUGE

Smooth work with your hands. Measure a shell surrounded by other shells.

1 shell knitted together with other shells = approx. 4¼ in / 11 cm in height and 8 in / 20 cm wide.

Adjust needle size to obtain correct gauge if necessary.

INSTRUCTIONS

Technique

This pattern is based on School 7 (page 134), and the diagram on page 141. Learn the technique by knitting all of the School 7 swatch, or only some of it.

Stitch Count

Pick up and knit 45 sts firmly and evenly. If you have more or fewer than 45 sts, adjust stitch count on Row 2 so there are 22 sts on each side of the center st (marked st). Work the rest as for School 7, Shell 1, from Row 2 on, but on jumper needle U. S. 4 / 3.5 mm.

SHAWL
PANEL 1

This is the first panel with 10 shells lying diagonally over each other.

Shell 1

Beginning shell—work as for School 7, Shell 1 with 45 sts.

Shell 2

A shell with 45 sts and cast-on at the left side.

Row 1 (RS), pick up and knit: Beginning at left before marker, with yellow, pick up and knit 22 sts along top of Shell 1's top left corner; turn and K-CO 22 sts = 45 sts.
Work as for School 7, Shell 1, beginning on Row 2.

Shells 3 to 19

Work as for Shell 2, over each other, as Shell 2 was worked over Shell 1.

Shell 10

Half shell, right half with 23 sts. The last st is Shell 9's end st (marked st).
Work as for School 7, Shell 2.

PANEL 2

Work to right of Panel 1.

Shell 11

A shell with 45 sts and cast-on at the left side.

Row 1 (RS), pick up and knit: K-CO 22 sts. Holding needle with sts in right hand, pick up and knit 1 st in Shell 1's right corner and 22 sts along top right side.
Continue as for Shell 1, beginning on Row 2.

Shell 12

Shell knitted between 2 shells

Row 1 (RS), pick up and knit: Pick up and knit 20 sts along top right side of Shell 19, k1 in end st of Shell 1 (marked st), and pick up and knit 22 sts along top right side of Shell 2.
Continue as for Shell 1, beginning on Row 2.

SHELLS 13 TO 20

Work as for Shell 12 along Panel 1.

Shell 21

Work as for Shell 10, but work last st of pick-up-and-knit row in end st of Shell 10 (marked st).

PANELS 3 TO 6

Work to correspond to Panel 2.

PANEL 7

Work as for Panel 6 until Shell 83 has been knitted.

Along left wing's top side (84, 85, etc): Use end st (marked st) from shell to right as next shell's first st, so the panel ends without any markers.
NOTE: Shell 82 is the center shell, from which the wings point out in opposite directions.

Shell 91

Use end st (marked st) from Shell 90 as first st and 75's end st (marked st) as last st. End when 6 sts rem after a WS row as follows:
Next Row: *Sl 1 pwise, k2tog, pass slipped st over knit st*; rep from * to * and end by passing back st over first.

PANEL 8

Work as for previous panels until Shell 97 has been worked.
Shell 98 is not worked into 82's end st, the first knitted with when the edging is worked.

PANEL 9

Work as for previous panels, but along top side of right wing (105, 112, etc): Use end st of shell to left as next shell's last st, so this side also is now without markers.

PANEL 10

Work as for previous panels, but 106 is a half shell.

A Half Shell (23 sts)

The left half of Shell 99's right tip

DIAGRAM FOR WING SHAWL

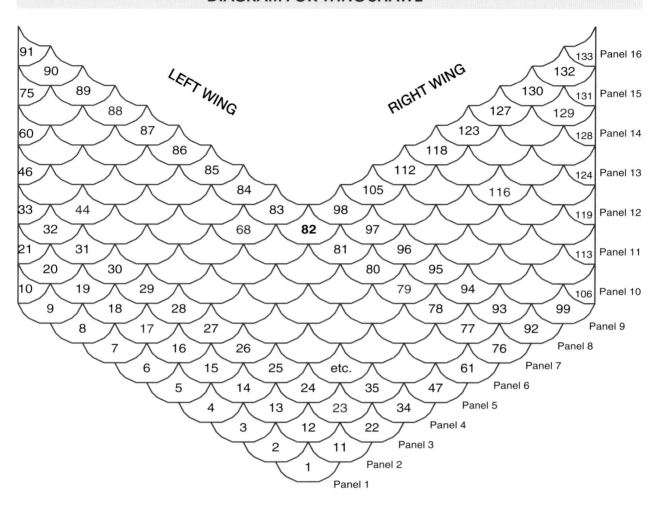

Colors

All shells with black numbers are worked with yellow.

Shells with red numbers are worked with the following colors:

Gray-violet: Shells 23, 44, and 114

Salmon: Shells 17, 88, 79, and 129

Light red: Shells 68 and 117

Overview

Beginning shell: 1

Shells with cast-on at left side: 2, 3, 4, 5, 6, 7, 8, and 9

Shells with cast-on at right side: 11, 22, 34, 47, 61, 76, 92, and 99

Half shells, right half: 10, 21, 33, 46, 60, 75, and 91

Half shells, left half: 106, 113, 119, 124, 128, 131, and 133

Shells knitted between 2 shells: all top shells

is 106's first st. Work rest of shell as
for School 7, Shell 7.

PANELS 11 TO 15
Work to correspond to Panel 10.

PANEL 16
Shell 133
The panel consists of only one half
shell.
Use end st of Shell 131 as first st
and 132's end st as last st.
End as for Shell 91.

FINISHING
EDGING
The edging is worked along the top
long side (right and left wings) with
yellow and 48 in / 120 cm U. S. 2.5
/ 3 mm circular, and same size dpn
to help. Use Garter Stitch Edging
with 2 Edge Stitches on page 181,
although here, there are special
points.

Ridges
Row 1 (RS), pick up and knit:
With yellow, pick up and knit 18 sts
along Shell 133, 22 sts along each
of next 8 shells along right wing,
1 st in 82's end st (marked st) and
pm on this st, 22 sts along each of
next 8 shells along left wing, and
18 sts along 91.
Row 2 (WS): Sl 1 pwise, knit to
end of row.
There is now 1 ridge on RS.
Place a stitch stopper on end of
circular where yarn is not hanging,

and use dpn to help with knitting
at other end of circular.

First Point
Row 1 (RS): Sl 1 pwise, k1; turn.
Row 2 (WS): Sl 1 pwise, k1; turn.
Row 3: Sl 1 pwise, k2; turn.
Row 4: Sl 1 pwise, k2; turn.
Row 5: Sl 2 pwise, k2; turn.
Row 6: Sl 1 pwise, k3; turn.
Row 7: Sl 2 pwise, k3; turn.
Row 8: Sl 1 pwise, k4; turn.
Row 9: Sl 2 pwise, k4; turn.
Row 10: Sl 1 pwise, k5; turn.
Row 11: Sl 2 pwise, k5; turn.
Row 12: Sl 1 pwise, k6; turn.

Garter Stitch Edging with 2 Edge Stitches
Row 13 (RS): Sl 2 pwise wyon, k4,
p2tog; turn.
Row 14 (WS): Sl 1 kwise, knit to
end of row = 7 sts total.
Rep Rows 13-14 until 13 sts rem
after a WS row = edging 7 sts + 6
of the sts picked up and knitted on
Row 1.

Last Point
Next Row (RS): Sl 2 pwise wyon,
k3, p3tog; turn.
Next Row (WS): Sl 1 kwise, knit to
end of row; turn.
Next Row: Sl 2 pwise wyon, k2,
p3tog; turn.
Next Row: Sl 1 kwise, knit to end
of row; turn.
Next Row: Sl 2 pwise wyon, k1,
p3tog; turn.

Next Row: Sl 1 kwise, knit to end
of row; turn.
Next Row: Sl 2 pwise wyon,
p3tog; turn.
Next Row: Sl 1 kwise, knit to end
of row; turn.
Next Row (RS): Sl 1 pwise wyon,
p3tog; turn.
Next Row (WS): Sl 1 kwise, k1;
turn.
Next Row (RS): Sl 1 pwise wyon,
k2tog, pass slipped st over knitted
st.
Finish off.

SHELL TOP

An unbelievably sweet summer top to wear with everything—and it is also fun to knit these lace row shells. The top is worked in one piece with shells arranged one over the other, primarily in panels slanting to the left. To finish—just seam the shoulders.

SIZES
S/M (L/XL)

FINISHED MEASUREMENTS
Chest: before washing, 40¼ (45) in / 102 (114) cm; after washing, 39½ (44) in / 100 (112) cm
Total Length: before washing, 15 (16½) in / 38 (42) cm; after washing, 17 (19¼) in / 43 (49) cm

MATERIALS
Yarn: CYCA #1 (fingering) Isager Bomulin (65% cotton, 35% linen, 230 yd/210 m / 50 g)
Yarn Colors and Amounts:
Light Yellow Green 40: 300 g
Each shell weighs approx. 2 g

Needles: U. S. size 1.5 / 2.5 mm: 8 in / 20 cm hybrid jumper needle, 24 in / 60 cm circular
U. S. size 0 / 2 mm: dpn and 24 in / 60 cm circular

Notions: locking ring stitch markers

GAUGE
1 shell = approx. 2⅜ (2½) in / 6 (6.5) cm in height and 5⅛ (5¾) in / 13 (14.5) cm wide. Measure Shell 5 after completing Shell 9. Adjust needle size to obtain correct gauge if necessary.

INSTRUCTIONS
Work following pattern below and diagram with overview of the various shells.

Technique
This pattern is based on School 7 (page 134), and the diagram on page 147. The shells for this top are a little different in that they have eyelet lace on Row 2.

Stitch Count
1 shell has 31 (35) stitches.

FRONT
Begin with part of the front.

Shell 1
Beginning shell.
Using short jumper needle, K-CO (with 2 beg sts) 31 (35) sts and work shell as follows:
Row 1 (WS): Knit.
Row 2 (RS), lace: Sl 1 pwise, k2tog, (yo, p2tog) to end of row = 30 (34) sts.

Hill

Row 3 (WS): Sl 1 pwise, k2tog, knit to end of row = 29 (33) sts.

Row 4 (RS): Sl 1 pwise, p2tog, purl to end of row = 28 (32) sts.

Row 5: Sl 1 kwise, k2tog, knit to end of row = 27 (31) sts.

Valley

Row 6 (RS): Sl 1 pwise, k2tog, knit to end of row = 26 (30) sts.

Row 7 (WS): Sl 1 pwise, p2tog, purl to end of row = 25 (29) sts.

Row 8: Sl 1 kwise, k2tog, knit to end of row = 24 (28) sts.

Continue as est, alternating hills and valleys (Rows 3-8) with fewer and fewer sts until 3 sts rem.

End with sl 1, k2tog, psso; place last st (= end st) on a locking ring maker. Weave in ends (photo A).

Shell 2

Shell with sts cast-on at left side. Begin to left of Shell 1's end st and pick up and knit 15 (17) sts along Shell 1's top left side; end with pick up and knit 1 st in Shell 1's outermost left cast-on loop; turn and K-CO 15 (17) sts = 31 (35) sts. Work as for Shell 1.

Shell 3

Work as for Shell 2: begin at left before Shell 2's end st.

Shell 4

Shell with sts cast-on at right side. K-CO 15 (17) sts. Holding needle with sts in right hand, pick up and knit 1 st in outermost right corner of Shell 1 and pick up and knit 15 (17) sts along Shell 1's top right side = 31 (35) sts.

Work as for Shell 1.

Later, work Shell 7 as for Shell 4.

Shell 5

Shell between 2 shells. Pick up and knit 15 (17) sts along Shell 4's top left side, k1 in Shell 1's end st and 15 (17) sts along Shell 2's top right side = 31 (35) sts. Work as for Shell 1.

Shells 6 to 9

Continue in numerical order following diagram; see also Overview.

Check Gauge

After completing Shell 9, it is time to check the gauge. Lay piece on a table, lightly pat it until it is fairly flat, and measure Shell 5. Continue if your gauge matches that of the pattern or change to larger or smaller needles as necessary.

Shells 10 to 16

Continue in numerical order following diagram; see also Overview. After completing Shell 16, set piece aside.

BACK

Work as for Shells 17 to 32 on front.

FRONT AND BACK, CONTINUATION

Join the two pieces with Shell 33 as follows:

Shell 33

Shell 33 is worked between 2 shells with a joining stitch in the center. Pick up and knit 15 (17) sts along

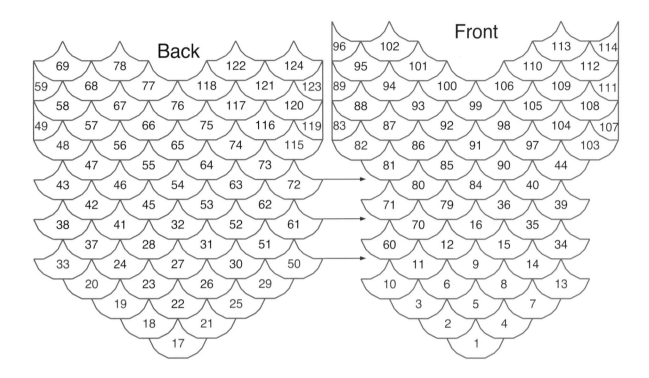

Diagrams

Make a copy of the two diagrams, cut them out, and tape them together with the tips on the front slotting into the notches on the back:

Shell 50 should sit over 10, etc.; see red arrow.

On the other side, 33 sits over 13, etc.

Shell 48 is taped together with 103.

Shell 82 is taped together with 115.

You now have a "mock-up" of the finished top, before the shoulders are joined.

Overview

Beginning shells: 1 and 17

Shells with cast-on at left side: 2, 3, 10, and 18, 19, 20

Shells with cast-on at right side: 4, 7, 13, and 21, 25, 29

Half shells, right half: 49, 58 and, 83, 89, 96

Half shells, left half: 107, 111, 114 and 119, 123

Shells knitted between 2 shells with a joining stitch in the center: 33 and 50

Shells knitted between 2 shells: All rem top shells.

top left side of Shell 20, insert needle through outer left cast-on loop of Shell 20 and then through Shell 13's outer right cast-on loop, knit the 2 loops together. Continue, picking up and knitting 15 (17) sts along top right side of Shell 13 = 31 (35) sts.

Shells 34 to 47

Continue in numerical order following diagram until Shell 47 is complete.

Shell 48

Work over Shell 47 as Shell 2 was knitted over Shell 1.

Shell 49

Right half of a shell with 17 (19) sts. K1 into end st of Shell 48, pick up and knit 15 (17) sts along Shell 48's top left side, k1 in 48's outer cast-on loop = 17 (19) sts (photo B).

NOTE: *Always* decrease *only* on RS rows.

Beginning

Row 1 (WS): Sl 1 pwise, knit to end of row.
Row 2 (RS), lace: Sl 1 pwise, k2tog (yo, p2tog) to end of row = 16 (18) sts.

Hill

Row 3 (WS): Sl 1 kwise, knit to end of row.
Row 4 (RS): Sl 1 pwise, p2tog, purl to end of row = 15 (17) sts.

Row 5: Sl 1 kwise, knit to end of row.

Valley

Row 6 (RS): Sl 1 pwise, k2tog, knit to end of row = 14 (16) sts.
Row 7: Sl 1 pwise, purl to end of row.
Row 8: Sl 1 kwise, k2tog, knit to end of row = 13 (15) sts.

Continue as est, alternating hills and valleys (Rows 3-8) with fewer and fewer sts until 3 sts rem.
NOTE: *Always* decrease *only* on RS rows.

End as follows:
Next Row (WS): Sl 1 pwise, p2.
Next Row (RS): Sl 1 kwise, k2tog.
Next Row (WS): Sl 1 pwise, p1.
Next Row (RS): Sl 1 k1, psso.

Shell 50

Work Shell 50 between 10 and 29, as for Shell 33.

Shells 51 to 81

Continue in numerical order following diagram; see also Overview.

Shell 82

Work Shell 82 over 81, as for Shell 48.

B

Shells 83 to 102

Continue in numerical order following diagram.

Shell 103

Shell with sts cast on at right side, above Shell 44.

K-CO 15 (17) sts. Holding needle with sts in right hand, pick up and knit 1 st in 43's end st. Pick up and knit 15 (17) sts along same shell's top right side = 31 (35) sts.

Work as for Shell 1.

Shells 104 to 106

Continue following diagram.

Shell 107

Half shell, left half with 17 (19) sts. Shell 107 looks like a mirror image of Shell 83 (or 49).

K1 in 103's outer cast-on loop. Pick up and knit 15 (17) sts along top right side of Shell 103 = 16 (18) sts.

NOTE: *Always* decrease *only* on RS rows.

Beginning

Row 1 (WS): Knit to end of row.
Row 2 (RS), lace: Sl 1 pwise, (yo, p2tog) to end of row until 2 sts rem, k1 p1.

Hill

Row 3: Sl 1 kwise, k2tog, knit to end last st, p1.
Row 4: Sl 1 kwise, purl to end of row.

Row 5: Work as for Row 3 = 15 (17) sts.

Valley

Row 6 (RS): Sl 1 kwise, knit to last st, p1.
Row 7: Sl 1 kwise, p2tog, purl to end of row = 14 (16) sts.
Row 8: Work as for Row 6.

Continue as est, alternating hills and valleys (Rows 3-8) with fewer and fewer sts until 3 sts rem. End as for Shell 49.

Shells 108 to 124

Continue until all shells have been knitted.

FINISHING

Left shoulder seam: Beginning at front neck, sew Shell 113 into arch of 69-78, then sew 69 to 114.
Right shoulder seam: Beginning at front neck, sew Shell 102 into arch of 122-124, then sew 96 to 124.

NECKBAND

Beginning at one shoulder between 101 and 122, on RS with U. S. 1.5 (2.5) mm circular, pick up and knit approx. 136 (144) sts around neck. Join and purl 1 rnd and then knit 5 rnds (stockinette on RS). Change to U. S. 0 / 2 mm circular and knit 5 more rnds.

BO very loosely. Fold band in half to WS and sew down.

SLEEVE EDGINGS

With U. S. 0 / 2 mm circular, pick up and knit 70 (80) sts around sleeve and purl 1 rnd. Knit 10 rnds in stockinette. BO loosely. Fold band in half to WS and sew down.

GARMENT CARE

When garment is finished, wash it as follows: Put top into washing machine with wool wash and cold water. If possible, use a no-rinse wool wash such as Eucalan, Soak, or Bommix (www.bommix.dk). After top has soaked, stop cycle and spin out at top speed. Hang top on a clothes hanger to dry so it will stretch lengthwise.

8
CIRCLES

CIRCLES

By using the fairly simple German short-row technique, you can turn in the middle of a row without making a hole. Short rows are used for shaping, and, in this case, to create circles with 16 segments that I call "birthday cake slices." The circles are knitted counter-clockwise.

FINISHED MEASUREMENTS

Diameter: 7 in / 18 cm

MATERIALS

Yarn: CYCA #3 (DK, light worsted) Filcolana Pernilla (100% pure new wool, 191 yd/175 m / 50 g)

Yarn Colors and Amounts:
Charcoal Heather 956 (charcoal): 50 g
Medium Gray Heather 955 (gray): 50 g
Acacia Heather 825 (curry): 50 g

Needles: U. S. size 2.5 / 3 mm: 2 dpn

SWATCH

Technique

Circle shaped with German short rows (see page 186). The circles are knitted counter-clockwise.

A circle is composed of birthday layer cake slices and each slice has a wide side and a narrow side.

The wide side: This side arches and is part of the circle's circumference—that is, the side with the most edge stitches. All subsequent slices begin at this side. It is also where the colors change, and where the yarn is carried up.

The narrow side: The left side, where the work turns, with the right side facing you as shown in photo A. This side forms the inside of the circle.

Changing Colors

The last-knitted stitch on the row on the side where the colors change is always purled and the next row begins with sl 1 kwise. Colors are always changed on the RS (the right side).

On the row with the color change, cross the colors **clockwise**, and *at the same time*, slip the first stitch knitwise.

If you want to carry up colors, end all rows at the side with the color change with p1 and begin next row with slip the first stitch knitwise, and *at the same time*, cross the colors **counter-clockwise** (photo C).

In photo D, you can see how the

charcoal yarn is carried up inside the edge stitches without pulling in the edge.

See also Changing Colors with stripes on page 174.

A CIRCLE

Birthday Cake Slice 1

Begin at arrow in photo A.

With charcoal and dpn, K-CO (with 2 beg sts), 20 sts.

Row 1 (WS), set-up row: Knit to end of row. There is now 1 ridge on RS. The first row is a set-up row/ridge, which is not included with the slice's ridge count.

Row 2 (RS), forward: Sl 1 pwise, k2; turn.

Row 3 (WS), return: DS (= pull up with working yarn so st flips and 2 legs are on needle; see page 186), k2.

There is now a tiny ridge of only 1 st on RS; the first st is an edge st and the last is a DS. It will be a bit difficult to see but it is counted in the ridge count.

Row 4, forward: Sl 1 pwise, k1, knit DS as 1 st, k2; turn.

Row 5, return: DS, knit to end of row.

Row 6, forward: Sl 1 pwise, knit to DS (here: k3), knit DS as 1 st, k2; turn.

Row 7, return: DS, knit to end of row.

Row 8, forward: Sl 1 pwise, knit to DS (here: k5), knit DS as 1 st, k2; turn.

Row 9, return: DS, knit to end of row.

Rep Row 8-9 with more and more

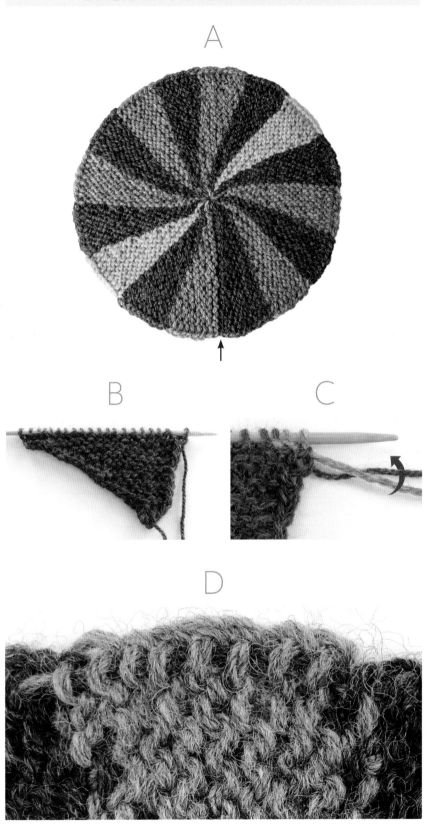

A

B

C

D

sts before the turn until 3 sts rem to the left of the DS and there are 16 sts to right after a return row on WS (= 20 sts). The working yarn and yarn end both hang at the wide/right side.

Row 18 (RS): Sl 1 pwise, knit to DS, knit DS, knit to end of row (= k3); turn.

Row 19 (WS): Sl 1 pwise, knit to last st, p1 (photo B).

The slice now has 9 ridges along the wide side (after the set-up row).

Birthday Cake Slice 2

Change to gray and carry charcoal up (see photo C).

*Row 2 (RS), forward: Sl 1 kwise, k2; turn.

Row 3 (WS), return: DS (= pull up with working yarn so st flips and 2 legs are on needle; see page 186), k1, p1.

Row 4, forward: Sl 1 kwise, k1, knit DS as 1 st, k2; turn.

Row 5, return: DS, knit to last st, p1.

Row 6, forward: Sl 1 kwise, knit to DS (here: k3), knit DS as 1 st, k2; turn.

Row 7, return: DS, knit to last st, p1.

Row 8, forward: Sl 1 kwise, knit to DS (here: k5), knit DS as 1 st, k2; turn.

Row 9, return: DS, knit to last st, p1.

Rep Row 8-9 with more and more sts before the turn until 3 sts rem to the left of the DS and there are 16 sts to right after a return row on WS (= 20 sts). The working yarn and yarn end both hang at the wide/right side.

Row 18 (RS): Sl 1 kwise, knit to DS, knit DS, k3; turn.

Row 19 (WS): Sl 1 pwise, knit to last st, p1.

The slice now has 9 ridges along the wide side (after the set-up row)*.

Birthday Cake Slices 3 to 16

Work as for Slice 2 from * to *. See colors on photo of circle on page 155. Gray and charcoal alternate, but Slices 6 and 14 are substituted with curry.

JOINING

Begin at the center and insert a needle through all 20 cast-on loops. Fold work with right sides facing with the cast-on row and live stitches held up and parallel. Join the sets of sts with three-needle bind-off from the outside to the center (see page 184). Do not cut yarn, but draw end through edge sts at center of circle; pull together. Cut yarn and weave in ends.

BOOMERANG SHAWL

A nice, cozy shawl you can't do without. It is warm, easy, and fun to knit, and can be worn in so many ways. The half circles at each end are connected by a straight section with a quarter circle in the middle to form a boomerang.

SIZE
One size

FINISHED MEASUREMENTS
Width: approx. 19 in / 48 cm

MATERIALS
Yarn: CYCA #3 (DK, light worsted) Filcolana Pernilla (100% pure new wool, 191 yd/175 m / 50 g)
Yarn Colors and Amounts:
Charcoal Heather 956 (charcoal): 250 g
Medium Gray Heather 955 (gray): 150 g
Acacia Heather 825 (curry): 50 g

Needles: U. S. size 2.5 / 3 mm: hybrid jumper needle, 24 in / 60 cm circular, 1 dpn,
Crochet Hook: U. S. size C-2 / 2.5 mm

GAUGE
25 sts and 54 rows/27 ridges in garter st = 4 x 4 in / 10 x 10 cm

INSTRUCTIONS
Technique
The pattern is based on School 8 (page 154), and photo A on page 161. Learn the technique by working the entire School 8 swatch or part of it.

All half circles in this pattern are worked **counter-clockwise**, so all forward rows are on the RS and return rows on WS. All color changes occur at right side of piece.

HALF CIRCLE 1
Birthday Cake Slice 1
Knit the slice as follows:
With curry and jumper needle, K-CO (with 2 beg sts), 60 sts.

Row 1 (WS), set-up row: Knit to end of row. There is now 1 ridge on RS. The first row is a set-up row/ridge, which is not included with the slice's ridge count.

*Row 2 (RS), forward: Sl 1 pwise, k2; turn.

Row 3 (WS): return: DS (= pull up with working yarn so st flips and 2 legs are on needle; see page 186), k2.

After Rows 2-3, there is now a tiny ridge of only 1 st on RS; the first st is an edge st and the last is a DS. It will be a bit difficult to see but it is counted in the ridge count.

Row 4, forward: Sl 1 pwise, k1, knit DS as 1 st, k2; turn.

Row 5, return: DS, knit to end of row.

Rep Rows 4-5, forward and return with more and more sts before the turn, until there are 3 sts to the left of the DS and 56 sts to the right. Work a return row, ending row with p1 (= 60 sts).

The yarn now hangs on the wide side where there are 29 ridges*.

Birthday Cake Slice 2

Change to gray.

Row 1 (RS): Sl 1 kwise, knit to DS, knit DS, k3.

Row 3 (WS): Sl 1 pwise, knit to end of row.

Continue as for 1st slice from * to *.

Birthday Cake Slices 3 to 6

Work as for Slice 2. Knit Slice 3 with charcoal, Slice 4 with gray, Slice 5 with charcoal, and Slice 6 with gray (photo B).

STRAIGHT SECTION

Now work a straight section over the entire diameter = 120 sts.

With charcoal and 24 in / 60 cm circular, work back and forth as follows:

Row 1 (RS), transition row: Sl 1 pwise, knit to end of row = k59. The yarn is now at center of half circle. With crochet hook to help, insert it into all 6 edge sts (only through the top loops) in the little arch in center of half circle, yarn over hook, draw through the loops to make 1 st and place st on needle; tighten and continue to pick up and knit 59 sts in Slice 1's cast-on loops. Pick up 1 st in the outermost edge st through both loops. There are now 121 sts, which is 1 st too many, but that st will be decreased away on the next row.

Row 2 (WS): Sl 1 pwise, k58, k2tog, knit to end of row = 120 sts.

Row 3: Sl 1 pwise, knit to end of row.

Row 4: Sl 1 pwise, knit to end of row.

Rep Rows 3-4 until the straight section measures 12¾ in / 32 cm (87 ridges on RS). End with a WS row, ending that row with p1.

QUARTER CIRCLE

This slice is worked on the same principle as the half circle, but the radius is twice as large, with twice as many stitches.

Large Birthday Cake Slice 1

Knit with curry.

Row 1 (RS) forward: Sl 1 kwise, knit to end of row.

*Row 2 (WS), return: Sl 1 pwise, knit to end of row.

Row 3: Sl 1 pwise, k7; turn.

Row 4: DS, knit to end of row.

Row 5: Sl 1 pwise, k6, knit DS as 1 st, k8; turn.

Row 6: DS, knit to end of row.

Row 7: Sl 1 pwise, knit to DS, knit DS as 1 st, k8; turn.

Row 8: DS, knit to end of row.

Rep Rows 7-8 until 8 unworked sts rem and there are 15 ridges on RS. The last row is on WS*.

Next Row (RS): Sl 1 pwise, knit to DS, knit DS as 1 st, knit to end of row.

Work from * to * once more. The last row is on WS and ends with p1. The yarn hangs at the wide side and there are 30 ridges on RS.

Birthday Cake Slices 2 to 9

Work as for Large Birthday Cake Slice 1, beginning on Row 1, alternating gray and charcoal slices.

STRAIGHT SECTION

Continuing with charcoal, work as for first straight section on all 120 sts, beginning with Row 3. The last row is on WS and ends with p1. Pm at center of row.

HALF CIRCLE 2
Birthday Cake Slice 1

Knit with curry as for Half Circle 1's Slice 1 from * to *, but begin Row 2 (RS) with sl 1 kwise.

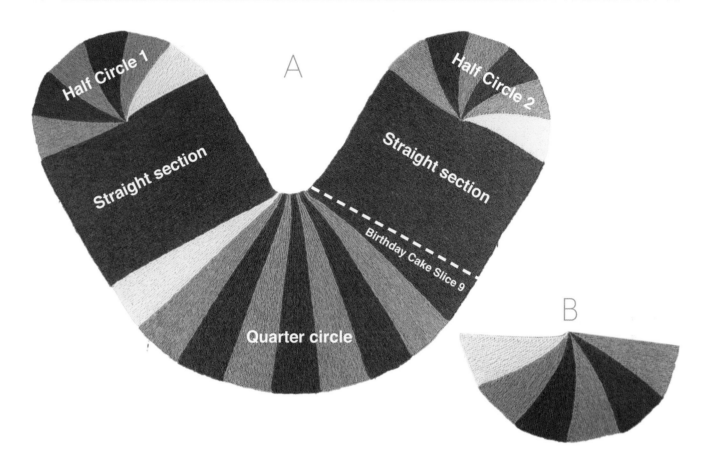

Birthday Cake Slices 2 to 6

Now work 5 slices as for the first, alternating gray and charcoal. End Slice 6 on RS at short side (in center of half circle).

Next Row (WS), joining row:

With crochet hook to help, insert it into all edge sts (only through the top loops) in the little arch in center of half circle, yarn over hook, draw through the loops to make 1 st and place st on circular; tighten and sl 1 pwise, k2tog, knit to last st, p1. Place charcoal st on jumper needle, so tip points away from center.

Fold half circle in over the straight section and BO with 3-needle bind-off.

SNAKE SCARF

You can arrange this scarf in so many different ways. It's fun to knit, and when it's finished, you can embellish the right places on your outfit and arrange it as needed to warm yourself. The scarf is composed of half circles or half "cake slices," knitted counter-clockwise. Each half circle has 7 birthday layer cake slices.

SIZE
One size

FINISHED MEASUREMENTS
Width: approx. 6¼ in / 16 cm

MATERIALS
Yarn: CYCA #3 (DK, light worsted) Filcolana Pernilla (100% pure new wool, 191 yd/175 m / 50 g)
Yarn Colors and Amounts:
Charcoal Heather 956 (charcoal): 100 g
Medium Gray Heather 955 (gray): 100 g
Acacia Heather 825 (curry): 50 g

Needles: U. S. size 2.5 / 3 mm: hybrid jumper needle 10 in / 25 cm, 1 dpn,
Crochet Hook: U. S. size C-2 / 2.5 mm

GAUGE
25 sts and 54 rows/27 ridges in garter st = 4 x 4 in / 10 x 10 cm

INSTRUCTIONS
Technique
The pattern is based on School 8 (page 154) and photo A on page 165.

Color Sequence
Curry (Small Half Circle 1), gray, charcoal, *gray, charcoal, gray, charcoal, curry*; rep * to * and end with gray, charcoal, gray, charcoal (Small Half Circle 2). See also photo A.

SMALL HALF CIRCLE 1
Work as for Birthday Cake Slices 1-7 in School 8, but all with curry. See photo B, where arrow shows direction of knitting. The yarn hangs on the wide/right side.

LARGE HALF CIRCLE 1
This half circle is worked as for the small half circle, but with twice as many stitches (40 sts) on jumper needle.
Continue in **counter-clockwise** direction.

Large Birthday Cake Slice 1

Begin by working a transition row with gray over Small Half Circle's Slices 7 and 1 as follows:

Row 1 (RS), transition row: Sl 1 kwise, k19. The yarn is now at the center of the slice.

With crochet hook to help, insert it into all 7 edge sts (only through the top loops) in the little arch in center of slice, yarn over hook, draw through the loops to make 1 st and place st on needle; tighten and continue to pick up and knit 19 sts in Small Half Circle's Slice 1 cast-on loops. Pick up 1 st in the outermost edge st through both loops. There are now 41 sts, which is 1 st too many, but that st will be decreased away on the next row.

Row 2 (WS): Sl 1 pwise, k18, k2tog, knit to end of row (= 40 sts).

Row 3, forward: Sl 1 pwise, k2; turn.

Row 4, return: DS (= pull up with working yarn so st flips and 2 legs are on needle; see page 186), knit to end of row (= k2).

Row 5, forward: Sl 1 pwise, k1, DS (work as 1 st), k2; turn.

Row 6, return: DS, knit to end of row.

Rep Rows 5-6 with more and more sts before the turn, until 3 sts rem before DS and 36 sts are to right of it after a return row on WS which ends with p1 (= 40 sts).

There are 19 ridges along the wide side where the working yarn and yarn end hang.

Counter-clockwise—all forward rows are on RS and return rows on WS.

Clockwise—all forward rows are on WS and return rows on RS.

Large Birthday Cake Slice 2

Knit with charcoal.

Next Row (RS): Sl 1 kwise, knit to DS, knit DS as 1 st, knit to end of row.

Next Row: Sl 1 pwise, knit to end of row.

Continue with short rows as for Large Birthday Cake Slice 1, beginning on Row 3 until there are 3 sts to left of DS and 36 sts to right after a return row on WS (= 40 sts).

There are 19 ridges along the wide side where the working yarn hangs.

Large Birthday Cake Slices 3 to 7

Work as for Large Birthday Cake Slice 2, continuing in color sequence.

LARGE HALF CIRCLE 2

This half circle is knitted **clockwise.**

Large Birthday Cake Slice 1

Knit with gray.

Row 1 (RS), transition row: Sl 1 kwise, knit DS, knit DS as 1

st, knit to end of row. End row by joining Large Half Circle 1's 7 center loops on left side (at red arrow on photo C) with crochet hook, as on Large Birthday Cake Slice 1 at start of pattern. There are now 41 sts, which is 1 st too many, but that st will be decreased away on the next row.

Row 2 (WS), forward: Sl 1 pwise, k2tog, k1; turn.

Row 3 (RS), return: DS, k2.

Row 4: Sl 1 pwise, k1, knit DS as 1 st, k2; turn.

Row 5: DS, knit to end of row.

Rep Rows 4-5 until 3 unworked sts rem.

Photo C shows the first 9 ridges.

Next Row (WS), forward: Sl 1 pwise, knit to DS, knit DS, knit to end of row.

There are 19 ridges along the wide side.

Large Birthday Cake Slices 2 to 7

Change colors, and don't forget to weave in ends as you knit.

Row 1 (RS), return: Sl 1 pwise, knit to end of row.

Continuing in color sequence, work as for this half circle's Large Birthday Cake Slice 1, beginning on Row 2.

Weave in all ends.

LARGE HALF CIRCLE 3

This half circle is knitted **counter-clockwise**, beginning with a couple of transition rows.

Large Birthday Cake Slice 1

Knit with gray.

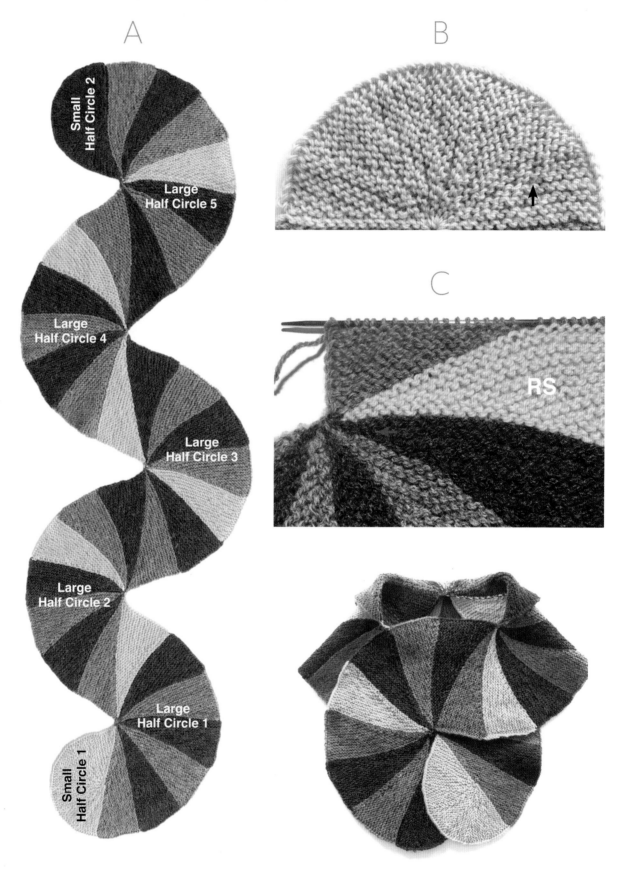

A

Small
Half Circle 2

Large
Half Circle 5

Large
Half Circle 4

Large
Half Circle 3

Large
Half Circle 2

Large
Half Circle 1

Small
Half Circle 1

B

C

RS

Row 1 (RS), transition row:
Use crochet hook to gather up the center sts from Large Half Circle 2 from bottom up and onto the free needle; k2tog, tighten work, and knit to end of row.

Row 2 (WS): Sl 1 pwise, knit to end of row.

Continue as for Large Half Circle 1's Large Birthday Cake Slice 1, beginning on Row 3, until there are 3 sts to left of DS and 36 sts to right after a return row on WS. The working yarn hangs to right of wide side (= 40 sts).

There are 19 ridges along the wide side.

Large Birthday Cake Slices 2 to 7
Continuing in color sequence, work as for this half circle's Large Birthday Cake Slice 1 (photo D).

LARGE HALF CIRCLE 4
Work as for Large Half Circle 2, **clockwise**.

LARGE HALF CIRCLE 5
Work as for Large Half Circle 3, **counter-clockwise**.

SMALL HALF CIRCLE 2
Large Birthday Cake Slices 1 to 7
Work **counter-clockwise**, in a single color (charcoal).
Row 1 (RS), transition row:
Sl 1 kwise, knit to DS, knit DS,

knit to end of row, ending row by gathering Large Half Circle 5's 7 center loops as on Large Birthday Cake Slice 1 from beginning of pattern. There are now 41 sts, which is 1 st too many, but that st will be decreased away on the next row.

Row 2 (WS): Sl 1 pwise, k2tog, knit to end of row.

Pm at center of row and leave the 20 sts on left needle to rest.

Now knit a small half circle over the 20 sts on right needle, as for Small Half Circle 1 = for School 8, Birthday Cake Slice 1, Row 2. End Slice 7's next-to-last row (at center) by gathering the half circle's loops with a crochet hook and knitting back: Sl 1 wise, k2tog, knit to end of row.

Place the 20 sts of Large Half Circle 5 on a dpn. Fold work with right sides facing so the 2 needles are parallel. BO with 3-needle bind-off in towards center of last half circle.

TECHNIQUES
AND
EDGINGS

BASIC TECHNIQUES

CASTING ON

Most cast-ons begin with a slip knot, but a book from 1875 described a way to begin with two beginning stitches and no knot. You can learn how to do this cast-on here. All the patterns in this book use this method for casting on.

CAST-ON WITH TWO STITCHES
= 2 beginning stitches

These 2 stitches are always a good way to begin whether you begin with a long-tail or knitted cast-on.

Hold the yarn as a bow in your left hand, with the yarn end over your thumb and the yarn from the ball over your index finger (photo A).

Insert needle tip over the bow (the yarn between your two fingers), and tip needle down and to the left (clockwise) so the yarn makes a loop around the needle (photo B).

Hold the stitch firmly on the needle with your index finger and cast on 1 stitch with the long-tail method.

A

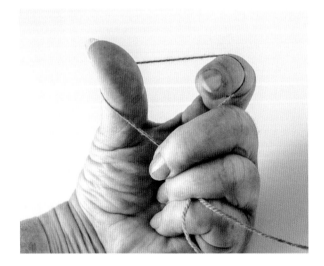

B

There are now 2 stitches on the needle (photo C).

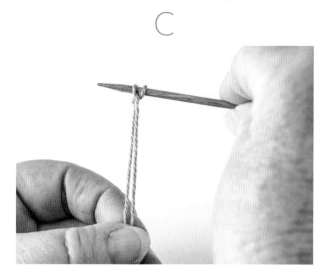

Tighten the stitches on the needle and you're ready to cast on more stitches.

When you've cast on with 2 beginning stitches, always end the first row with knit 1 through back loop (twisted knit).

LONG-TAIL CAST-ON

The long-tail cast-on is the most common method for casting on in Denmark because those who learned how to knit in school learned this method as the easiest one.

For this cast-on, hold one needle in your right hand and the yarn in the left. For more details, look for videos on YouTube.

KNITTED CAST-ON
= K-CO

The knitted cast-on is used throughout this book. If you are not familiar with this method, you should learn it. You can try it with my guidance here, but you can also find videos demonstrating it on the internet.

Use two needles and some yarn.

Whether you're casting on for the beginning of a project, or have one already in progress, or you have just cast on the first 2 stitches (as on page 170), hold the needle with a stitch or some stitches in your left

hand and hold a free needle in your right hand.

Begin where the yarn hangs. The outermost stitch in your left hand is the beginning stitch.

*Knit the first (beginning) stitch but leave the "old" stitch on the left needle.

Draw out the new stitch a bit and place it, twisted, over the needle in your left hand (photo D).

There is now 1 stitch more on the left needle. Leave right needle in stitch; tighten yarn*.

Repeat from * to * until you've cast on the desired number of stitches (photo E).

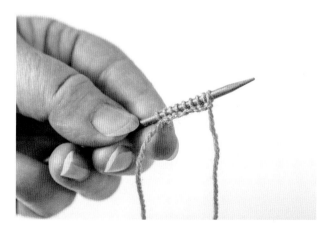

DECREASES

There are two methods of decreasing that look almost alike, but

P2tog is worked on the **right side** (photo F) while

Sl 1, k1, psso is worked on the **wrong side** (photo I).

PURL 2 STITCHES TOGETHER
= p2tog

You might wonder why you purl stitches together when decreasing on the right side. It's actually quite logical. Think about ribbing—knit 1, purl 1, for example, in which the purl stitches hide between the knit stitches. It is exactly that look that you exploit when you purl 2 together on the right side. The purl stitches simply hide and are not seen in the finished project.

As seen on right side: The decrease with p2tog lies very flat (photo G).

As seen on wrong side: This decrease lies like a stockinette stitch on the wrong side (photo H).

SLIP 1 PURLWISE, KNIT 1, PASS SLIPPED STITCH OVER
= sl 1, k1, psso

With yarn held under/behind needle (wyun/wyb), slip 1 stitch as if to purl, knit 1, pass the slipped stitch over the knitted stitch. This can be worked in one easy movement: insert needle into stitch as to purl (and leave stitch on needle), knit next stitch, take needle back through first stitch (from left to right), and let both stitches slide off needle.

When 2 stitches need to be joined on the wrong side, I work, sl 1, k1, psso.

As seen on right side: Sl 1, k1, psso looks like a little fold (photo J).

As seen on wrong side: This decrease also lies like a stockinette stitch with a little fold on the wrong side (photo K).

In use and after washing, these 2 decrease methods will look alike.

AFTER DECREASING

If you've worked p2tog, slip first stitch knitwise after a turn.

If you've worked sl 1, k1 psso, slip first stitch purlwise with yarn over needle after a turn.

F

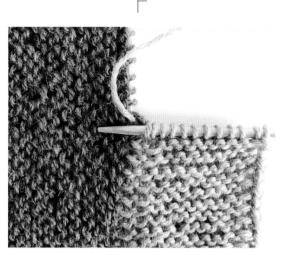

Decreasing with p2tog on right side.

I

Decreasing with sl 1, k1, psso on wrong side.

G

Finished decreasing with p2tog as seen on right side.

J

Finished decreasing with sl 1, k1, psso as seen on right side.

H

Finished decreasing with p2tog as seen on wrong side.

K

Finished decreasing with sl 1, k1, psso as seen on wrong side.

CHANGING COLORS WITH STRIPES

Change colors on the right side so you'll have a clean shift, without the colors mixing.

Always end with purl 1 on the row before a color change and when the colors will be carried up. This purl stitch allows the color change to lie smoothly on the wrong side of the work, when the first stitch of the next row will be slipped.

NARROW STRIPES—THE COLORS CROSS

Always cross the colors at a color change as follows:
For a smooth color change that won't draw in the work, the colors must be twisted **clockwise**:
The color used below (here, white), is drawn in towards you and up over the last used color (here: turquoise); place yarn over index finger, ready for knitting (photo L).
Make sure that the work does not pull in at the side with the color changes.
The swatch shows the color change on every other row, where the edge stitch looks like one and a half stockinette stitches (photo M).

WIDE STRIPES—THE COLORS ARE CARRIED UP

When there are more than 2 rows between color changes, it is advantageous to bring the colors up invisibly on the wrong side before the next color change, without drawing in the work. To do this, the colors must cross each time a right side row begins, as follows:

Twist colors counter-clockwise, so the color to be knitted with (here: white) comes in towards you, down and around the "old" color *(here: turquoise); continue with the same color as before (photo N).
You can see the wrong side here where the turquoise yarn lies inside the edge stitches (photo O).
This shows the right side, where the turquoise yarn can just be sensed (photo P).

L

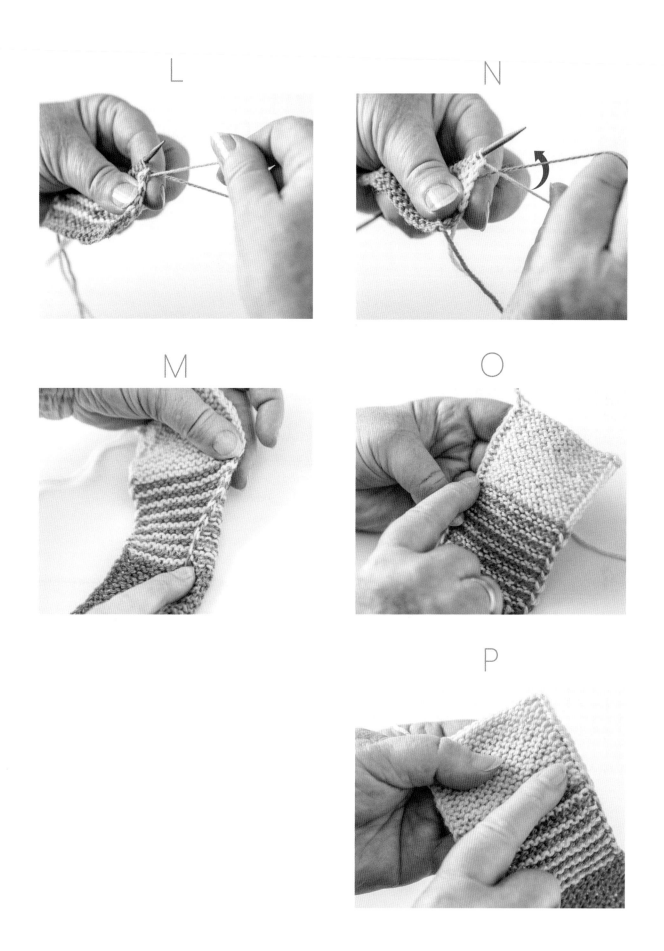

M

N

O

P

WEAVING IN ENDS

This section offers two methods for weaving in ends, both of which have the same elasticity as the knitted work.

WEAVING IN AS YOU KNIT

Most knitters have to weave in ends. Don't forget to do it! If you weave in most ends as you knit, there won't be many ends to weave in later with a needle.

End the last row before a row for weaving in with p1.

From Right to Left

Hold yarn (2 strands) over fingers as for Norwegian pattern knitting (2-color stranded colorwork) as follows:

The color to be woven in (O = old color) is held innermost over the index finger and the color to be knitted with (N = new color) is held first, nearest fingertip over 2 fingers: index and middle fingers.

Insert needle into stitch, **under** O and around N, and knit stitch with N.

Now insert needle into stitch, **over** and around O and N, and knit stitch with N.

Repeat these two steps as long as you think necessary but only when knitting on right side.

On the right side, the weaving in will be invisible, but it will look like a little snake slithering across the wrong side (photo Q).

More On Weaving In As You Knit

Always weave in the lowest end first. Then you can weave in the end which now hangs lowest, etc.

Do not trim ends right away. First, knit a couple of rows after weaving in, and then trim ends to about ⅜ in / 1 cm. If you trim to close to the work, the end could slip out onto the right side when you wash the piece.

From Left to Right

Ends on the left side can be pulled to the right and woven in the same way. After a couple of rows, you can pull in the loop that pokes up.

Over how many stitches should you weave in? It depends; I usually weave in over 13-17 stitches.

WEAVING IN ON THE DIAGONAL

To avoid too many confusing yarn ends, I recommend that you weave in ends while the stitches are still on the needle so you have something to hold onto.

Weaving in on the diagonal is almost invisible, and is as elastic as the knitted piece.

In garter stitch, it's best to weave in on the diagonal on the wrong side—that is, into every single little loop (photo R).

The work won't pull in and the weaving cannot be seen on right side of work (photo S).

If weaving in 2 strands that hang at the same place between 2 figures (see photo D on page 36), I join them with a single knot before I weave them in. That holds the figures together.

A ridge looks like it consists of small S-twists in a row. Insert the needle into the first S-twist and then into the next S-twist, and so on, to the next ridge, etc.

Q

R

S

EDGINGS

Good edgings for jackets, throws, and other items are indispensable. The edgings put a perfect finishing touch on a project. Did you know that a sweater knitted on U. S. 2.5 / 3 mm needles can have somewhere in the neighborhood of 65,000 stitches? So you can certainly take a few hours or days to work an edging and properly complete a project you've invested so much effort into, right?

It's a good idea to work a sample of an edging you think you want to use before you begin knitting it around a large piece of work.

When you knit an edging on a large project, you can work back and forth on 2 needles. If you want to use a circular, work back and forth with the circular in one hand and a double-pointed needle in the other. I put a stitch stopper on the unused end of the circular (see pages 11 and 185), and that way I can use it to push the stitches together. It is also often an advantage to use a needle smaller than that used for the main project—usually by one U.S. size / half mm—for the edging.

A GARTER STITCH SQUARE

This square is knitted as the beginning part of all 4 edgings.

With dpn U. S. 2.5 / 3 mm, K-CO 20 sts.
The edge stitches should be firm and uniform as the basis for the edge which will later be knitted onto it.

Row 1 (WS): Knit to end of row.
Row 2 (RS): Sl 1 pwise, knit to end of row.
Row 3(WS): Sl 1 pwise, knit to end of row.
Rep Rows 2-3 until there are 19 ridges on RS and 20 ridges on WS.
BO on WS. Now there are 20 ridges on both RS and WS.

GARTER STITCH EDGING WITH 1 EDGE STITCH

An easy and pretty edging that can be used on many items. First, knit a ridge in a contrast color, and then a garter stitch edging, with 1 edge stitch and a corner shaped with short rows.

MATERIALS
Yarn: CYCA #3 (DK, light worsted) Filcolana Pernilla (100% pure new wool, 191 yd/175 m / 50 g)
Colors and Amounts:
Marzipan Heather 977 (natural white)
Cantaloupe Heather 826 (salmon)
Nougat Heather 973 (gray-brown)

Needles: U. S. size 2.5 / 3 mm: dpn and 16 in / 40 cm circular

Square
With natural white, knit a garter stitch square as described on page 179.

Ridges
Row 1 (RS), pick up and knit:
With salmon and circular, beginning in lower left corner of square, pick up and knit 20 sts on RS into base (in cast-on loops), 1 st in corner loop (pm here), 20 sts along right side and 1 extra st in top right corner.
Row 2 (WS): Sl 1 pwise, k2tog, knit to end of row.

Garter Stitch Edging with 1 Edge Stitch
Change to gray-brown and K-CO 6 sts as an extension of row (in lower left corner). Knit with circular in one hand and dpn in the other.
Row 1 (RS): K5, p2tog; turn.
Row 2 (WS): Sl 1 kwise, knit to end of row.
Row 3 (RS): Sl 1 pwise, k4, p2tog; turn.
Rep Rows 2-3 until just before corner.
Point
Turn corner with German short rows (DS, see page 186).

Row 1 (RS): Sl 1 pwise, k4; turn.
Row 2 (WS): DS (pull stitch so it flips over and now there are 2 legs on needle) knit to end of row.
Row 3: Sl 1 pwise, k3; turn.
Row 4: DS, knit to end of row.
Row 5: Sl 1 pwise, k2; turn.
Row 6: DS, knit to end of row.
Row 7: Sl 1 pwise, k1; turn.
Row 8: DS, knit to end of row.
Row 9: Sl 1 pwise, knit the 2 legs of DS tog as one st; turn.
Row 10: Knit to end of row.
Row 11: Sl 1 pwise, k1, knit the 2 legs of DS tog as one st; turn.
Row 12: Knit to end of row.
Row 13: Sl 1 pwise, k2, knit the 2 legs of DS tog as one st; turn.
Row 14: Knit to end of row.
Row 15: Sl 1 pwise, k3, knit the 2 legs of DS tog as one st; turn.
Row 16: Knit to end of row.

Garter Stitch Edging, Continuation
Row 17: Sl 1 pwise, k4, p2tog; turn.
Row 18: Sl 1 pwise, knit to end of row.
Rep Rows 17-18 until all salmon sts have been eliminated after a RS row. End with BO, slipping 1st st.

GARTER STITCH EDGING WITH 2 EDGE STITCHES

This edging begins almost the same way as the Garter Stitch Edging with 1 Edge Stitch, but it has 2 edge stitches and the corner is folded. It makes a nice pocket for a pillow or blanket.

MATERIALS
Yarn: CYCA #3 (DK, light worsted) Filcolana Pernilla (100% pure new wool, 191 yd/175 m / 50 g)
Colors:
Aqua Mist Heather 808 (turquoise)
Fisherman Blue Heather 818 (dark blue)
Granite Heather 812 (gray-blue)

Needles: U. S. size 2.5 / 3 mm: dpn and 16 in / 40 cm circular

Square
With turquoise, knit a square as described on page 179.

Ridges
Row 1 (RS), pick up and knit:
With dark blue and circular, beginning in lower left corner of square, pick up and knit 20 sts on RS into base (in cast-on loops), 1 st in corner loop (pm here), 20 sts along right side and 1 extra st in top right corner.
Row 2 (WS): Sl 1 pwise, k2tog, knit to end of row.

Garter Stitch Edging with 2 Edge Stitches
Change to gray-blue and K-CO 7 sts as an extension of row (in lower left corner). Knit with circular in one hand and dpn in the other.
Row 1 (RS): Sl 2 pwise, k4, p2tog; turn.
Row 2 (WS): Sl 1 kwise, knit to end of row.
Rep Rows 1-2 until just before corner.

Corner Fold
Row 1 (RS): Sl 2 pwise, k5; turn.
Rep Row 1 a total of 13 times. The last row is on WS.
Fold edge out and up and move sts from dpn to circular.

Garter Stitch Edging, Continuation
Continue edging as before corner, until only 1 dark blue st rem after a WS row.
BO, sl 2 pwise, pass the one st over the other, k1 and BO as usual, ending with k2tog before passing last st over the joined st.

I-CORD EDGING

An I-cord edging knitted around a piece is a lovely, simple finishing touch. Knot the cord at the corners for an extra flourish.

MATERIALS
Yarn: CYCA #3 (DK, light worsted) Filcolana Pernilla (100% pure new wool, 191 yd/175 m / 50 g)
Colors:
Oatmeal Heather 978 (gray-beige)
Fisherman Blue Heather 818 (dark blue)

Needles: U. S. size 2.5 / 3 mm: dpn and 16 in / 40 cm circular

Square
With gray-beige, knit a square as described on page 179.

I-Cord Edging
Row 1 (RS), pick up and knit:
With dark blue and circular, beginning in lower left corner of square, pick up and knit 20 sts on RS into base (in cast-on loops), 1 st in corner loop (pm here), and 20 sts along right side. Cut yarn.
Go back to place where Row 1 began. Hold the work in your left hand with WS facing you, and with dark blue and dpn in right hand, K-CO 4 sts as an extension of cast-on sts.
Row 2 (WS): With second dpn, k3, p2tog, leave yarn on index finger, while dpn is inserted into first st on circular (= with yarn under needle), sl st and push dpn to left and ready to knit.
Row 3 (RS): Using free dpn, k3, p2tog, leave yarn on index finger, while dpn is inserted into first st on

circular (= with yarn under needle), sl st and push dpn to left and ready to knit.
Rep Row 3 until just before corner, ending with p2tog. There are now 4 sts on right needle.

Knot in Corner
Hold yarn over index finger and dpn behind work and push needle to the left.
Now work without joining cord to square: K4 and push needle to left. Rep this row until cord is about 2 in / 5 cm long—long enough for a firm knot.
Place sts onto locking ring marker and tie a knot without cutting yarn.

I-Cord Edging, Continuation
Return sts to dpn and continue as before knot, beginning with Row 2 until 5 sts rem (4 I-cord sts and 1 st from pick-up-and-knit row).
BO, and *at the same time* p2tog with last I-cord st and last pick-up-and-knit row st.

RIBBED EDGING

As for the Garter Stitch Edging with 1 Edge Stitch and Garter Stitch Edging with 2 Edge Stitches, this edging begins with a contrast-color ridge. The edging is worked in k1, p1 ribbing with increases to round the corners.

MATERIALS
Yarn: CYCA #3 (DK, light worsted) Filcolana Pernilla (100% pure new wool, 191 yd/175 m / 50 g)
Colors:
Nougat Heather 973 (gray-brown)
Acacia Heather 825 (curry)
Willow Heather 822 (khaki)

Needles: U. S. size 2.5 / 3 mm: dpn and 16 in / 40 cm circular

Square
With gray-brown, knit a square as described on page 179.

Ridges
Row 1 (RS), pick up and knit:
With curry and circular, beginning in lower left corner of square, pick up and knit 20 sts on RS into base (in cast-on loops), 1 st in corner loop (pm here), 20 sts along right side, and 1 extra st in top right corner.

Ribbed Edging and Corners
Change to khaki and begin at top at bind-off so first row is on WS. The stitch count on both sides of the corner stitch should be an even number.
Row 1 (WS): Purl.
Row 2 (RS): K1 (edge st), (p1, k1) to corner st, 1 e-inc, k1, 1 e-inc, (p1, k1) to end of row.
Row 3: (P1, k1) to corner st, p1, (p1, k1) to end of row.

Row 4: K1 (edge st), (p1, k1) to corner st, 1 e-inc, k1, 1 e-inc, (k1, p1) to end of row.
Row 5: (P1, k1) to corner st, p1, (k1, p1) to end of row.
Row 6: K1 (edge st), (p1, k1) to corner st, 1 e-inc, k1, 1 e-inc, (p1, k1) to end of row.
Row 7: (P1, k1) to corner st, p1, (k1, p1) to end of row.
BO in ribbing.

KNITTING HELP

In this section, you'll find explanations for techniques often used in this book. You can find more information and instructions for all of these techniques by searching the internet and YouTube.

SLIP 1 PURLWISE
= Sl 1 pwise
Insert needle, under yarn, into stitch as if to purl (i.e., into stitch from right to left); move stitch, under yarn, to right needle without working it.

In this book, sl 1 pwise always means: slip the stitch with the yarn held over the needle (wyon) unless the text explicitly says wyun—with yarn held under needle. See more in Abbreviations.

SLIP 2 PURLWISE
= Sl 2 pwise
Insert needle, under yarn, into 2 stitches as if to purl (i.e., into stitches from right); move stitches, under yarn, to right needle without working them; tighten slightly (photo A).

A

3-NEEDLE BIND-OFF
Hold two needles in your left hand with the sets of stitches parallel and the needle tips pointing to the right.

Using a third needle, k2tog, joining the first stitch of each needle (insert needle knitwise into stitch on front needle and then into first stitch on back needle). *K2tog with next 2 front stitches; pass back stitch on right needle over first stitch*. Rep * to * until all stitches have been bound off.

BINDING OFF IN KNIT OR PURL
Bind off (BO) knitwise: You will most usually bind off knitwise, even when text only says "bind off." If you are meant to bind off purlwise, the text will state that explicitly.

CROCHET TOGETHER
See Joining with Crochet.

EDGE STITCHES
= edge st(s)
Begin with sl 1 pwise when last row ended with a knit stitch.

Begin with sl 1 kwise when last row ended with a purl stitch.

Always tighten second stitch. That little tug makes the edge stitches neat, firm, and tight.

PICKING UP STITCHES

When picking up stitches, it's more important to avoid holes in the work than to pick up exactly the right number of stitches. If you have too many or too few stitches when you're done picking up, you can always adjust the stitch count on the next row.

Knit

In this book, unless otherwise specified, when the text says "pick up xx number of stitches," it means: Pick up and **knit** xx number of stitches: hold work with right side facing you, insert needle from front, **always into both loops** of an edge stitch, and with yarn held below needle, knit 1.

Purl

You can also pick up and purl stitches. When the text says "pick up and purl xx number of stitches," it means: Hold work with wrong side facing you, insert needle from back in under an edge stitch and, **always under both loops**, with yarn held over needle, purl 1 (photo B).

B

RIDGES

It doesn't matter whether you knit all the rows or purl all the rows; they will produce ridges. When you knit, a ridge stands up on the back of the work, and when you purl, the ridge appears on the front.

JOINING WITH CROCHET

Two pieces can always be knitted together, but a crochet hook makes the work easier. Don't forget to crochet loosely so the join will have the same elasticity as the knitting. Join with crochet **slip stitches**: *Insert hook through nearest stitch (edge stitch, cast-on loop, or stitch) and continue through back stitch, yarn over hook (= catch yarn around hook) and draw yarn through both stitches and then through loop on hook*. Repeat from * to *. When crocheting through edge stitches, insert hook through both loops, but for cast-on loops, go through only 1 loop. When crocheting through a knitted stitch, insert hook through stitch.

STITCH STOPPERS

When knitting back and forth on a circular with many stitches, and when knitting a few stitches near one end only, I use a stitch stopper (see photo on page 11). I place the stopper on one end of the circular (the end not in use) and push the stitches together with the stopper. Then I can knit with the circular in one hand and a "helper" needle in the other.

BEGINNING STITCH
= beg st

As you've seen under Knitted Cast-on on page 171, the knitted cast-on in this book begins with 2 stitches. These stitches are called beginning stitches. A beginning stitch can also be a new stitch, the first stitch on a needle, or only a loop, picked up somewhere in the knitted fabric. Often the end stitch of a figure is the beginning stitch for the next figure.

GAUGE

The gauge for a project is always listed with the materials and other information necessary before you begin knitting. The gauge is usually given as a number of stitches and rows in 4 x 4 in / 10 x 10 cm.

Always check your gauge **before** you begin the actual project.

Knitted Swatch

Cast on the number of stitches recommended for the gauge plus 2-3 extra stitches at each side.

Knit the swatch straight up—making it somewhat larger than 4 in / 10 cm in each dimension—and measure it.

If your gauge is not the same as given in the pattern, you must try smaller or larger needles and knit a new swatch. If the gauge then matches, you can get started on the project.

In this book, you will also find another type of gauge listed in some of the patterns; for example, staircases measured by the width and height of a step.

Check the gauge—not only before you begin but as you work. Gauge can change as you work or when there are too many stitches on the needle.

SIZES

Most of the patterns in this book are given for one size only. They can, however, easily be adjusted, because stripes, squares, tri-squares, right angles, steps, and shells can have more or fewer stitches, and ridges can be larger or smaller. This way, both the width and length can be changed to stay in proportion.

INCREASES

M1 = make 1 = 1 lifted strand (twisted knit)

Lift strand between two stitches onto left needle and knit into back loop for a twisted knit.

1 inc = 1 lifted strand increase (knit)

Lift strand between two stitches onto left needle and knit into front loop for a knit stitch with a tiny hole.

E-Increase = e-inc

Twist the yarn around your index finger like an "e" and place the e on right needle like a stitch (photo C).

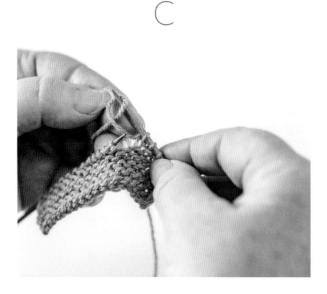

SHORT ROWS

There are several methods for working short rows. Different methods are used for different things, but all have the goal of avoiding holes when turning.

Short rows with wrapped stitches

On page 54, you can learn how to work with wrapped stitches, in which the yarn is wrapped around a stitch when the row is turned.

German short rows

One very good method for making short rows when turning is to use German short row turns with a **double stitch (DS)**. It is an easy method that doesn't leave any holes.

DS: Work to the turn; turn and make a DS (= slip first stitch purlwise with yarn held in front (over needle), tug working yarn so the stitch flips and two legs are now on the needle. See photo D. Work to end of row.

Working a double stitch: When you later come to a double stitch (DS), work both legs together as one stitch.

When counting stitches, always count a DS as one stitch.

Purling loosely or firmly

Many knitters purl more loosely than they knit. You might want to work the purl rows on a smaller needle when working stockinette, for some projects, but you can't do that in most of the patterns in this book. Instead, I recommend that you tug the yarn slightly with your left index finger after a purl stitch. That way, you'll have firmer purl stitches.

D

SLEEVES
Sleeve Length
The sleeves for both jackets in this book are worked from the top down, which allows you to easily adjust their length.

YouTube
If you want more details about how to make German short rows, search for "German short rows" on YouTube; you'll find plenty of helpful videos.

Use the knitted cast-on so there will be good elasticity at the edge you'll later sew into the armhole. End when the length suits you, but wait to add the edging. Finish knitting the jacket with edgings and finishing. Sew sleeves into armholes and seam sleeves from the top down, leaving the bottom open for about 4 in / 10 cm. Now try on the jacket and adjust the sleeve length before knitting on the sleeve edgings.

Increases and Decreases

When I decrease or increase on a sleeve, I knit a little rubber band together with the decrease or increase. I leave all the rubber bands on the piece. That makes it easy to see which ones are decreases or increases, and you can quickly count how many decreases/increases have been made and make sure your stitch count is correct. See photo E.

When the sleeve is finished, you can cut off the rubber bands.

E

ABBREVIATIONS

1 inc	lift strand between two stitches and knit into front (do not twist) strand; makes a small hole (see page 186)		p	purl
			pm	place marker
			psso	pass slipped stitch over
beg st	beginning stitch(es)		puk	pick up and knit
BO	bind off (= UK cast off)		pwise	work or slip as if to purl
cm	centimeter(s)		rem	remain(s)(ing)
CO	cast on		rep	repeat
dpn	double-pointed needles		rnd(s)	round(s)
DS	double stitch = 2 legs in German short row turning (see pages 186-187)		RS	right side
			sl	slip
e-inc	"e" increase—see page 190		sl 1, k1, psso	with yarn under (= wyb) needle, slip 1 st purlwise, k1, pass slipped st over
est	established			
in	inch(es)		sl 1, k2tog, psso	with yarn under (= wyb) needle, slip 1 st purlwise, k2tog, pass slipped st over
k	knit			
k2tog	knit 2 together (right-leaning decrease)		sl 1 kwise	slip 1 st as if to knit, wyb (see page 184)
k2-in-1	increase by knitting 2 stitches into one: knit 1, leaving st on left needle, knit into same st through back loop, slip st off left needle		sl 1 pwise	slip 1 st as if to purl, wyf (see page 184)
			sl 2 pwise	slip 2 sts as if to purl, wyf (see page 184)
			st(s)	stitch(es)
K-CO	knitted cast-on (see page 171)		tbl	through back loop
kwise	work or slip as if to knit		tog	together
m	meter(s)		wr st	wrapped stitch—(see page 50)
M1	Make 1 increase: lift strand between two stitches onto left needle and knit into back loop to twist strand		WS	wrong side
			wyb (wyun)	with yarn held in back of work or yarn held under needle (wyun)
mm	millimeter(s)		wyf (wyon)	with yarn held in front of work or yarn held over needle (wyon)
			yd	yard(s)
			yo	yarnover

YARN INFORMATION

CaMaRose yarns may be purchased from US retailers listed by:
Camarose
camarose.dk

Filcolana yarns may be purchased (with international shipping charges) from:
KNiTT Ltd
knitt.co.uk

Hedgehog Fibres yarns may be purchased from US retailers listed by:
Hedgehog Fibres
hedgehogfibres.com

Isager Strik yarns may be purchased from US retailers listed by:
Isager Strik
isagerstrik.dk

Some yarns may be difficult to find. A variety of additional and substitute yarns are available from:
Webs—America's Yarn Store
75 Service Center Road
Northampton, MA 01060
800-367-9327
yarn.com

LoveKnitting.com
loveknitting.com/us

If you are unable to obtain any of the yarn used in this book, it can be replaced with a yarn of a similar weight and composition. Please note, however, the finished projects may vary slightly from those shown, depending on the yarn used. Try www.yarnsub.com for suggestions.

For more information on selecting or substituting yarn, contact your local yarn shop or an online store; they are familiar with all types of yarns and would be happy to help you. Additionally, the online knitting community at Ravelry.com has forums where you can post questions about specific yarns. Yarns come and go so quickly these days and there are so many beautiful yarns available.